Madonna King is one of Australia's most accomplished journalists, having worked at senior levels at News Limited and the ABC, where she presented the *Mornings* programme in Brisbane for six years. Madonna writes for Fairfax's *Good Weekend*, has a highly successful weekly column for the *Brisbane Times* and has a regular radio spot on Brisbane's 4BC. She has written seven books, all defined by her skilful reporting and her ability to get people to talk in depth. Madonna is also a parent of two girls who are fast approaching the magic age of 14.

madonnaking.com.au
🐦 @madonnamking

ALSO BY MADONNA KING

MADONNA KING

BEING 14

First published in Australia and New Zealand in 2017
by Hachette Australia Pty Ltd

First published in Great Britain in 2019
by Headline Home
an imprint of Headline Publishing Group

1

Cover design by Christabella Designs
Cover photograph courtesy of Getty Images

Typeset in 12.2/18.6 pt Sabon LT Std by Bookhouse, Sydney
Printed and bound in Great Britain by Clays Ltd, Elcograf S.p.A.

Cataloguing in Publication Data is available from the British Library

ISBN 978 1 4722 6767 2
eISBN 978 1 4722 6768 9

HEADLINE PUBLISHING GROUP
An Hachette UK Company
Carmelite House
50 Victoria Embankment
London EC4Y 0DZ

www.headline.co.uk
www.hachette.co.uk

To all the mums in my life, but especially my own,
Rita King.

Contents

Preface

'You can have my granddaughter if you
like ... while she's 14, she's yours.'

Why write a book on 14-year-old girls? It's a question I've been asked by almost everyone who has not had one. The need for it became clear to me a couple of years ago, while facilitating a conversation with a panel of school leavers. I asked the Year 12 students to articulate the advice they would give to their younger sisters about secondary school. What were the biggest challenges they would be forced to navigate once they first arrived at their high school? They responded in chorus, along these lines:

'Warning: Year 9 is hard.'
'Skip Year 9 if you can.'

'Being 14 is the worst year possible.'
'Stay off social media when you turn 14.'

It caught me off guard and, with two daughters still deep inside Tweenie Land, set off a warning that there was something about the age of 14 that warranted attention. About a week later I received a text from one of my closest friends. 'I am warning you now: do not let your girls turn 14,' she said. Her daughter – a clever, sassy school leader – was 14.

What was this about? A week turned into a month, and I had the trifecta of concerns about 14-year-old girls. While addressing a group of about 100 people at a restaurant on the topic of writing biographies, I was asked what the content of my next book might be. 'I don't know,' I said honestly, 'but I'm thinking there's something about 14-year-old girls that needs to be talked about.' The heckle from the back of the room was as loud as it was unexpected. 'You can have my granddaughter if you like,' an elderly woman bellowed. 'She was a darling at 13, and I'd like to have her back at 15 – but while she's 14, she's yours!' Later, she told me how the family's 'golden girl' had turned into an 'evil princess', backchatting her parents, locking herself in her room, and pulling out of her music lessons. Her parents were lost and didn't know what to do.

Driving home, the synergy of those three messages stuck. In the space of a month I'd been alerted to something about 14-year-old girls by a panel of 17-year-old students, a 45-year-old mother and an 80-something-year-old grandmother. Intrigued, it set me on a path that led to this book.

Almost 200 14-year-old girls allowed me into their world as part of this research. They were chosen randomly, after approaching schools and associations, but together, the 192 teens straddled city and country areas, public and private and girls-only and co-educational schools. While the identities of those students and their schools have been protected by pseudonyms, a tidy picture emerged quickly of a generation of teens wrestling with where they fit – at school, in friendship groups, and even in their own families. They admit to feeling conflicted, constantly. They want to be the strong, independent young women their teachers encourage them to be. At 14, they've never had so many examples of leadership: they've witnessed a female prime minister in Australia, and women leading the United Kingdom, Germany and the International Monetary Fund. But they still find themselves bending to the demands of bullies in their class, or boys who want to go one step further. Some days turn into big sticky morasses.

A generation ago, a 14-year-old girl might have found herself in a familiar muddle: no longer a girl and not quite a woman. She'd have had a foot in both camps, and the chasm in between might have been brimming with conflict:

from a wavering self-esteem to an obsession with the latest fad; from rolling her eyes at her mother's request for a hug, to wanting an embrace, desperately, but not knowing how to ask. For this generation, however, so much is different. Social media follows her to bed each night, as fallouts with friends take on a crisis pitch. A 14-year-old girl today has a crying need to fit in with her friends – and will change what she believes in to do that – and an anxiety fuelled by pressure to look good, and think smart. Unlike previous generations of 14-year-old girls, she will be more connected than ever, in one way, and less connected in another. On some days, inside the packed school grounds, she will feel utterly alone amongst hundreds of others. She'll fight nastiness, mood swings, and be pressured to take risks that she knows she shouldn't. A toxic junk culture, alien to her mother's generation, will also challenge her mind and her body. She'll want boundaries, as much as she wants to test every one you set. Her passion will be boundless, and she'll jump to volunteer for a cause. And then she'll turn around and slam the door on her little sister, for no other reason than she was standing next to it. She'll drag her feet one moment, and skip along another, as long as no-one is looking.

In the pages that follow, you will meet girls who have had their identity stolen, and police who reveal that their jaws dropped when they were made to listen to the lyrics girls sing along to on the way to school.

You'll meet wonderful principals and teachers and school nurses, parenting experts and teen psychologists, all of whom are spending their days navigating a safe path for our 14-year-old daughters. You will hear that Kids Helpline has been contacted over 22 000 times in the past four years by 14-year-old girls. And like me, you might rashly dismiss that cohort as being children from 'troubled' homes: teenagers who live on the fringe. Many, if not most, are not. They are 14-year-old girls like Claire and Ann and Jo and Sarah who need help telling their parents about the B+ they scored, instead of the A expected. Or they might be an A student who has begun to self-harm, but her parents don't know. They might be the girl from the bus stop you drive past who is weighed down with the pressure of parental expectation, or a friendship fallout that has wrecked her self-confidence. They might be your daughter, or the daughter of your best friend.

Hundreds of books have been written about teen girls from the perspective of youth counsellors and teachers and psychologists. I'm none of those. And there is no doubt, too, that teen boys go through a difficult patch on the way to becoming men. But as a journalist, and a mother of two young daughters, I started this task wanting to understand how teen girls think, and how we respond. Teachers, principals, teen psychologists, school nurses and police all told me that 14-year-old girls were their 'biggest clientele'. Of course it could be 13-year-olds, or those just turned 15. But being 14, and in Year 9, was the eye of the storm. Why? Why not 10-year-old girls? Or older teens? Why do smart, sassy 14-year-old girls feel so lost? What do they see as their challenges? Do they believe that we understand the pickles they find themselves in? And what, if we were really listening, without judgement, would they want us to know?

'Even though I'm smiling [it] doesn't mean I'm happy with the world or myself.' - CLAIRE

'I don't know who I am anymore.' - POLLY

'I find myself saying stuff like "the world isn't fun anymore" a lot.' - JUSTINE

'It's a time of sadness and constantly feeling you are being judged. There are so many expectations.' - ROSE

'It's good and bad. At this age it is known that friendships change, which kind of sucks. Also, things are happening to your body and it begins to drain you. But being 14 can also be fun.' - ANN

'Being 14 is absolutely horrible. It is when (at least for me) you start to question everything and your life starts to crumble.' - EMILY

'Many teachers claim that Year 9 is the year students go savage.' - JODIE

'It's difficult. Can you tell us whether we're supposed to be adults or kids? 'Cause sometimes we're treated as one, and then the other.' – ALISON

Of course, being 14 can be a golden time too. You might see your daughter more passionate than ever, and wanting to volunteer to make the world a better place. You will see the beginnings of an awesome young woman, with an open heart and wanting the best for herself and everyone around her. If you have a daughter, you'll probably even see yourself. But my goal, from the outset, has been to give a voice to the nation's 14-year-old girls. They deserve to be heard. Their hope is that we will listen.

Being 14

'Being 14 sucks.'

TESSA,
14

Marise McConaghy, principal of Victoria's Strathcona Baptist Girls' Grammar School, has been explaining 14-year-old girls to their parents for decades. Previously deputy principal at Brisbane Girls' Grammar School, McConaghy says thinking of them as constantly on the drug LSD can help explain many of their actions. 'People who use this drug are apparently intense, changeable, internal, often cryptic or uncommunicative and of course dealing with a distant reality,' McConaghy told one big crowd of Year 9 parents. 'The emotional system is immature in early adolescence, and small events can trigger enormous reactions. A negative comment about appearance, or a bad mark on a test, can hurl a girl into a despair which can last days or minutes, and a new pair of jeans or a block of chocolate can elicit unparalleled bliss.'

The description will ring true for many parents of a 14-year-old girl. 'Teenage girls are extremists who try to see the world in black and white but end up over-analysing the grey,' McConaghy says. 'One affront can mean that they have no friends, or all the teachers hate them. Life is either marvellous or not worth living, school is either pure torment or is the best place on earth, teachers are weird psychos or okay, and they either love themselves and can't stop looking in the mirror or pathetic failures with no friends and loser, socially disastrous parents.' The thing is, the girls themselves don't understand the daily lurch between this and that, between needing their parents and eschewing them at every opportunity. 'They are sensitive and tender-hearted, mean and competitive, superficial and idealistic. They are confident in the morning and overwhelmed with anxiety by nightfall. They rush through some days with wild energy and then collapse, unspeaking, into lethargy for hours in front of the television. One minute they love their world and their families and friends, the next they are critical of everyone and dispirited and hopeless. Much of their behaviour is unreadable,' McConaghy says.

Being 14 is all of those things and more. Born in the first few years of this century, a 14-year-old might not have seen a 'dial-up' phone, outside of an antique shop. Hers is a world of touch screen and wifi, of devices and apps, of television on demand and music in the pocket, of instant gratification and connectivity. Respected social researcher Mark McCrindle refers to them as the up-agers because they're older, younger. 'The technology gives them access to things earlier, which from an educational perspective can be fantastic,' he says. But it means it can also send them into a world of bullying and social exclusion, where the power of celebrity reigns, and where 24-hour connectivity can rule their lives, dominating their sleep patterns and academic results, determining their friendships, and how they see themselves. This technology has been so transformative, McCrindle says, that it has left this cohort without a real view of the history behind them. 'Everything is in the now. Everything is being rebased from the 21st century, from the new era, the new economy,' he says. This group of teen girls has only ever known a world where there are more university students who are female than male, where authority and hierarchies and even chivalry are dead. But feeding the contradictions, it could also be the first generation in more than a century that doesn't expect to live better than their parents' generation, according to top economist Saul Eslake; a world where they will live under a ceiling of debt, built by their parents, and where productivity growth is permanently slower and job rotation faster. Home ownership will be hard, without an inheritance, but business opportunities, at the touch of a flatscreen, will feed the innovative from the comfort of their home desk. Childhood is already shorter than it's ever been, and the junk culture they face positively Brobdingnagian.

But many of the paradoxes facing 14-year-olds are generated not by external forces but by the contradictions of their own developing brains. Associate Professor James Scott, from the University of Queensland Centre for Clinical Research, says the ages from 12 through to 25 are crucial in the brain's development. A child and adolescent psychiatrist, Scott explains that the connections from one part of the brain to another become more efficient from the bottom to the top and from the front to the back, in that order. The older parts of the brain, at the bottom, drive biological needs, like hunger and reward and fear and emotion. These are the parts that mature early. The frontal cortex – the newer parts – help us organise and plan things. These keep our behaviour in check and ensure we consider the consequences of what we might do. These parts govern our judgement and reasoning powers, our self-regulation, logic and impulse. 'They make us stop and think, "Is this a really good idea or not?"' Scott explains. A 14-year-old will have the mature part of the brain working, but the frontal part will still be developing. 'So when you see kids do really silly things and think, "How could they do such a stupid thing?" – up to young adults

– part of the reason is that they have these adult drives that little kids don't have but they don't have the adult reasoning and logic and foresight yet to understand the consequences. This is the frontal cortex – which gives the teenager the reasoning skills,' he says. 'Someone might say, "Why is my 14-year-old so disorganised?" That's because that part of the brain's not developed yet.'

Associate Professor Alan Ralph from the Triple P Positive Parenting Program says the changes in the brain that occur between the ages of 12 or 13 and 25 mean we should keep in mind our expectations of what teens are able to do. 'One day you have a 14-year-old who is 25 and the next day you have one who is five, so you have to adapt your behaviour and that's a real hassle for parents. What I would say is to try to treat them as an emerging adult all the time. Sometimes it isn't going to work; they're going to be behaving like primary schoolers again. That doesn't mean you should change the way you respond to them. If you can be consistent in how you behave you should find that those ups and downs become flatter.' Of course, teens develop at different times too, and an adolescent's brain will be remodelled along the way, at different stages for different individuals. Girls' brains are also more likely to develop before boys' brains. But the stage is set. Even before our 14-year-old girls get out of bed each morning, they're often hamstrung by a brain that's still waiting for a maturity spurt.

The girls admit to feeling the enigma. They say they're up and down, happy then snappy. Being 14 is bittersweet; perfect one minute, pathetic the next.

'Being 14 is confusing and a mix of emotions. Sometimes you want to lock yourself in a room for years and some-times it's the most carefree and fun time you could ever imagine.' - OLIVIA

'Being 14 is a weird in-between age. I feel constantly conflicted about decision-making.' - PARIS

'We're not young and we're not old. We are kind of stuck in the middle. Like a middle child.' - SASHA

'We're the nothing year. Those below us don't respect us and those above us don't think we earn their respect. We're stuck in the middle, waiting to be treated seriously.' - BROOKE

A compelling homogeneity enveloped the girls' answers to questions ranging from their relationships with their parents to their biggest fears, from their use of social media to the influence of friends. Their responses were also similar when asked how they viewed the age of 14 and how their lives differed from those of their mothers, and even what they wanted their parents to know but couldn't bring themselves to reveal. Many of the issues they nominate as their daily challenges stand out to us, as adults, too: the pervasive influence of social media; falling out with friends; pressure to fit in, at any cost; unexplained anxiety. The list goes on. But surprises, at least for me, popped up too. Author and co-founder of *The Huffington Post* Arianna Huffington has been warning about an epidemic in sleeplessness – and these girls confirm that. They are so tired, many of them are learning nothing in the classroom. The teen craze that sees about one-third – according to teachers, principals and police – of 14-year-old girls sending a naked selfie to someone else is also an alarm bell for every parent. And before you pass over that, they will often be the A-student; the good girl in class who wants to push the boundaries in a way she thinks will not catch her out. That issue alone has given Jon Rouse, the head of Australia's Task Force Argos – which tracks down online sex predators – a daily headache, with parents and daughters pleading with him to remove photographs that have found their way onto an overseas website. He tells them there's nothing he can do; once it's been sent, a photograph can end up anywhere. But perhaps the biggest surprise, at least to me, was the queue outside the office of school counsellors, or the flood of calls to Kids Helpline, by A-grade students, scared to tell their parents they failed to get into the extension class in English or Maths or Science. They'd failed, in their view, because they'd only managed an A minus.

Alex Curtis, Kids Helpline Counselling Centre Supervisor, says 14-year-old girls are a big client group of the counselling service, and she wishes they would love themselves a little bit more. 'They're trying to find where they fit, and what strikes me is they seem to have this real need to please their parents,' she says. 'They call saying, "I'm worried they're going to be disappointed in me," or "I just want more time with them." It seems to be a real stage in their life where they are struggling with their own identity and independence but they still want that connection with Mum and Dad.' Senior Constable Kelly Humphries, a school-based police officer in the region between Brisbane and the Gold Coast, agrees. 'Fourteen. They are my problem children,' she says. 'They're trying to find their place, and it's the age where you can tell quite quickly whether a tomfool will turn into a seasoned offender.'

Parents agree that there's something about being 14. One big UK study of 2000 mothers and fathers, with children aged over 18, found 14-year-old daughters more troublesome than the terrible twos, which had previously held the crown. Helene Hardy, a school-based youth health nurse in Queensland, takes a deep breath when she's asked to describe today's 14-year-old girl. Girls of this age are regular visitors to her office, usually over a breakdown in a relationship (sometimes with her boyfriend but usually with her girlfriends). They feel disconnected from their parents, saying they're too busy for a long conversation. 'They're in the same house, but they are not connecting at all,' she says. Social media has taken their place, and night and day her chat with friends will send her to giddy heights, and toss her into pits of despair. These girls will search for a tribe, and their loyalty to that group – whether it's the TCs (the Too Cools), the Nerds or another group – will be absolute; a pack mentality even stopping her from speaking up when she knows something is wrong. 'It's happened forever,' Hardy says. But once upon a time, it didn't follow you home. 'They're actually finding school a safer place,' she says. Hardy tells the students to block bullies, usually other girls in the same year. '"You mean, turn my phone off?"' They're aghast at the suggestion. It's their company, their lifeline, even on the worst days.

Alan Ralph from Triple P says parents of teenagers might struggle with four issues that didn't exist in their earlier parenting. First, the arrival of puberty and the hormonal changes that come with that. Secondly, their teen's increased exposure to the world in terms of influence, and the fact that their (the parents') ability to control those influences is dramatically reduced. Thirdly, how to manage the push for independence that invariably comes with adolescence. And finally, the issue of brain development.

To the girls, their parents are both their best friends and their daily enemies. They need boundaries and butt up against every one of them. And parents, according to almost every expert I talked to, sometimes just give up. Exhaustion takes hold, along with a false hope that stepping back will bring the return of that tight bond of a few years ago. Susan McLean, who was a member of the Victoria Police for 27 years and authored *Sexts, Texts and Selfies*, calls that 'limp lettuce' parenting. She says while some parents sit in the corner with their fingers crossed, others are so overbearing they will ban all social media, with neither attitude helping their children in the long run. Those overbearing parents also make life a living hell for some school principals and teachers. Increases in school fees and a competitive education system mean parents have a bigger stake in the game, and teachers tell stories of parents threatening to take out AVOs against other students or parents, sending legal letters over friendship fights, and appealing over marks that amount to 0.05 per cent.

Karen Spiller, former principal of St Aidan's Anglican Girls' School in Brisbane, says Year 9 girls have always been a challenge. 'It's a tough time because they don't know who they are,' she says. 'They don't want to be like their mum. They want to be like whoever the latest pop star is. But for some of them, they have that cognition that they do actually want to be like their mum. They just don't want to admit it.' Full of potential, their energy is delightful, Spiller says, but they live in a whirlpool of ire and doubt, stuck between the security of childhood and the lure of young adulthood. They're trapped, and they feel it. 'They've got pressure from their parents. They have pressure from their school. Pressure from the boyfriend or the peer group – which is the ultimate. And they're in this really tough place.'

Spiller has been a strong public advocate for girls in education, and her desk is laden with self-help books on teen girls. 'Your daughter comes out of that 14-year-old tunnel,' she says. 'Eventually.' She sees it often: poorly behaved students who wear leadership badges in Year 12. Spiller might even have been one of them herself. 'I've got to say, I was pretty naughty in Year 8,' she says. 'I was at a large school . . . I don't know what I was doing, but I'd climb out windows and be rude to teachers who let me be rude to them. Teachers who weren't strong enough. Then, if the deputy principal was walking around the school, I'd be so terrified. In my heart of hearts I knew I wanted to be a good kid but I was playing on the fringes of being naughty.'

It's not a beat-up, school-based nurse Helene Hardy says. Year 9 can change your trajectory. 'From my experience, that's the age. It can make you tougher. I've seen some young people who have had a crap time of it but have done okay. Then I see other kids who just crumble.' It's a tunnel through to adulthood, where teen girls need to be guided to the exit signs, and their parents need to venture in at every entry sign they spot. Flo Kearney, former principal of Somerville House, a big independent school in Queensland with almost 1400 students from pre-prep to Year 12, and now CEO and head of Women's College at the University of Queensland says in her experience each girl's journey will be different. 'We had many mums at Somerville House who had two or three or four daughters. Each of them was different in the way they approached things, and even though the expectations are the same in any given family, you'll get a different response because they are different children.' Interestingly, a girl's experience through Year 9 will also depend on the particular cohort of students she is with. But Kearney says educators can often spot those girls who will fare better right at the start of Year 9. They will be the more mature of the cohort; they will carry a strong self-confidence, and a sense of self-containment into the playground. They will still push the boundaries and answer back, and often even struggle with themselves, but they will respond to the challenges in a way that doesn't pull them into a year-long quagmire,' she says. Dr Judith Locke, a clinical psychologist and author of *The Bonsai Child*, says those who cope well are more likely to be the girls who 'just get on with it'; they have a grit and a resilience and a confidence that they will cope. Locke says parents can encourage that, by not pandering to their children or going in to bat for them at every opportunity.

The pursuit of Little Miss Perfect, where 14-year-old girls feel the need to excel across the board – academically, in sport, the arts, and socially – is also driving an epidemic in teen anxiety. Death tops their worries, as they navigate a world where spot fires of terrorism dominate the news. Eating disorders, for this batch, are on the wane, according to teachers, but have been replaced by self-injury, an alarming trend where girls are using blades to harm themselves. They then hide it, pulling down their skirt or the sleeve of their shirt. Don't make a judgement here on who might be a candidate; experts claim it is widespread across many different personalities. Attacked for being self-absorbed and self-involved, some 14-year-old girls opt to feel pain as they travel the road to physical, emotional, intellectual and social adulthood.

'If you do one thing you are called a name and if you don't you are called the opposite. Whatever road you take, most of the time it won't end well.' - ROSE

'Fourteen is hard. You are trying to make friends with guys so it will help you in the long run. But you need to keep school, work, play and social life at an equal ratio.' - ABBY

'It's a struggle but a fun wild ride of emotions. Your body changes, but personally I love it.' - REBECCA

'I don't ignore my parents but I just don't keep the conversation going. If they ask me about school, I'll just give them a blunt answer.' - MILLIE

'Mum doesn't like me to shut the door, which gets me annoyed. I want to get away from everyone. And that means she doesn't trust me. She says *she does, but that shows she doesn't.'* - LAURA

Many 14-year-olds will sink into anonymity. These are, often, those 14-year-olds who are not 'the sporty girls' or the 'academics' or 'the dancers'. They're not the TCs (Too Cools), nor the class nerds. It's a year of division, says one Year 9 teacher, where girls are separated, inadvertently, into those who 'achieve' and those who don't. That latter group can lose their voice amongst the class stars, and become lost themselves. Bewildered parents will struggle to find the compass setting to help them find their way back.

That describes a world alien to their parents' teenage years, when technology was primitive and easily controlled, when we addressed our neighbours as Mr and Mrs and never by their first name, and where mistakes could be made freely, without the world knowing and commenting on it. Now, for a 14-year-old girl, the chance of a new reputation is virtually impossible. There is no starting over. They can move schools, as many have, but by the time they walk through the new school gate, everyone knows them, and why they have moved. Bullying and friendship fallouts and the pressure to fit in doesn't stop at the school lunch table; it follows them home, 24 hours a day, seven days a week, and spreads like wildfire through other schools, and suburbs. The empowerment promised feels false, and while they can text and sext into the early hours of the morning, one slip-up can shroud their reputation for years.

Dannielle Miller, co-founder and CEO of Enlighten Education, says we need to celebrate more the achievements of our female teens. She cites 14-year-old Jade Hameister, the youngest person in history to trek to the North Pole, but says wonderful small achievements by 14-year-olds regularly slip under the radar because of the media's negative focus. It's difficult to argue with that point. Think of the last news story you heard that related to 14-year-old girls. On the day I am writing this, there are two: an all-in brawl in a school ground between two 14-year-old girls over a social media comment, and the search for a 14-year-old girl who has not contacted her parents for several days. Miller says this group of girls comprises the nation's biggest volunteers, particularly with animals, and will be quick to sign up for 40-hour famines, readathons and doorknock appeals. 'They give back to the community in all of those ways, so despite the rhetoric about them all being rather narcissistic and more interested in selfies, they are really interested in community and helping and caring. They have a sense of optimism [and] they think they can help change the world. That's a really lovely thing about them.'

Fran Reddan, principal of Mentone Girls' Grammar School in Victoria, says issues around inequality are at the top of their mind. In a group of ten 14-year-old students, she found homelessness, the growing use of ice as a drug on some city streets, race relations, religion, refugees, human rights and terrorism were all current affairs issues that they felt strongly about. 'And the question they ask me is, "What is Australia doing?"' That's the exact reason, as a teacher, author, educator and parenting expert, that Maggie Dent loved standing in front of a Year 9 classroom. 'I chose that year because it's incredibly gutsy, passionate, evolving, and when you get to have the conversations with them you see the world through another lens that you've completely forgotten. They are easy to inspire. Easy to enthuse. Easy to fire up because they're so easily influenced,' Dent says. Principal of Loreto College in Adelaide Dr Nicole Archard argues that we need to not only celebrate girls more, but be alert to the language we use to describe them. 'Too often we sell it as a negative,' she says. 'Too often we sell it as "girls of that age are bitchy". Girls at that age aren't bitchy. It's just another label that we apply that is a gendered term.' The former dean of academic studies at Sydney's Wenona School, Archard says all the challenges 14-year-old girls face can be navigated more easily if they understand themselves, and build confidence, resilience and self-efficacy. 'Girls have to believe they can be leaders. It's not just providing them with role models and developing their skills. They've got to have that internal belief that they belong there, that they can fit there and that they have the capacity to do those things.'

Caroline Paul, author of *The Gutsy Girl: Escapades for Your Life of Epic Adventure*, says we parent our daughters very differently from how we parent our sons. 'When you look around you can hear it: parents telling their girls to watch out, or not to do that, or "no". We think we are protecting them but I really think we are limiting them,' she says. 'We've actually coupled fear and femininity, and we need to decouple them. We encourage fear in girls because we think it protects them. It's become so insidious that we just expect it. Nobody worries when a girl screams at a spider or lets somebody pick up a heavy object or refuses to bike down a steep hill. Yet if a boy did that we'd really worry for his future. So my question is, why aren't we worrying for a girl's future?'

Put that scenario of the spider, or careering down a hill on a bicycle, to a group of mothers, and they accept that there's a real variance in how they treat our sons and daughters. Certainly, in this group of mothers of 14-year-old girls, meeting on a sunny Wednesday afternoon, the chatter is full of mea culpas.

'It is partly our fault because we teach them to stand up and have an opinion and then . . .' – JULIE

'We had a comment from a friend once and she said her husband was cracking it about the daughter backchatting. And I said, "Well, you want her to go to a good strong school that teaches women's rights and being independent" – and then he gets home and tries to squash her.' – BARB

'What can we expect? You can't have your cake and eat it too.' – ANGE

And there seems nowhere where the 'having your cake and eating it too' is more difficult than in your 14-year-old's social media world.

Being connected

'They think they're talking to this really hot 17-year-old and they're not. It's the father of one of the girls.'

A POLICE OFFICER,
investigating a known paedophile.

Thinking of the following story takes me back to a shopping centre, a few years ago, when my four-year-old went missing. Every mother, perhaps every father, has a similar tale: the alarm that is followed quickly by a sick feeling, deep in the pit of your stomach; the nausea only held down by screaming her name, in the hope she hears. It's a gut-wrenching physical reaction, that dissipates quickly when she runs towards you, her arms outstretched.

Kellie's story had the same impact on me. It unfolded as she sat on the floor of her holiday house bedroom, tears messing with the mascara she'd applied meticulously only minutes ago; the result of a good deal she saw online. She narrowed her eyes, reading the text message again, as her tears turned the characters all wrinkly. By now, Kellie knew the words in the text off by heart. It was from a friend, accusing her of being hateful to her and their group of 14-year-old friends. Kellie didn't understand. She'd found this group of friends – her gang, as she called them – months earlier, and it's where she fitted. The angst that had filled her mornings with dread, as she passed through the school gates, had disappeared into their embrace, and she'd do anything for this group of girls. She'd never abuse any of them. Ever. And now, one of them was blaming her for nasty Facebook posts that attacked each of her friends, by name. Kellie called another friend, who promptly hung up on her. And another. On holidays, and without wifi, she couldn't access the Facebook page, but she knew someone else was behind the vitriol she was alleged to have ignited. As Kellie tells it, the panic started deep down in her stomach and kept growing and growing. She wanted to vomit. And that's when she collapsed on the floor, sobbing.

Kellie's story is common. In some cases, it follows a teen lending their phone to someone else, unaware of how it will be used against them, or when the author posts under another teen's name. In other cases, an open Instagram or Snapchat or even Facebook account might invite forgery. In an alarming number of cases, it's as wilful as it is spiteful. An ex-friend with a gripe will set up a fake account, with a photograph taken from the internet or scanned from a school magazine, and become the author of cruel taunts. 'I hate you, and so does everyone else,' she might write. 'Everyone wants you dead,' one of the girls I interviewed was told. 'You're a fake-ass ho and retarded and a bitch,' another was told. Or it might be less abusive, but just as unkind: 'We're all going into town after school on Thursday. All of us. Except you.' Or the heartbreak might be in response to a soured girl–boy relationship, where a simple 'no' to a school dance invitation forces the starter gun on a lengthy campaign, using a fake identity, to embarrass, goad and mock someone.

Ask a 14-year-old girl, and many of them have their own story. Says Kate, 'They [she doesn't know who] send me screen shots of what other people are saying about me – like I'm a cow – but I can't see who it is from, so at lunchtime I never know if I'm sitting next to the person who hates me. I don't even know why they do it, but it makes me hate school.' Tara agrees. 'Some people called me fake, and I know that doesn't sound bad, but if you don't know who it is, it makes you suspicious of all your friends. And now I don't have any friends.' 'Go kill yourself' is not an uncommon text penned to a 14-year-old. Sometimes it carries the link to websites to assist. 'You're fat.' 'Nobody likes you.' Mary tells of a recent request to follow from a friend. 'So I did, and then these revolting photographs of her came up. It wasn't her account. Someone had hacked her and then uploaded all this stuff.'

Often, the fake accounts are easy to track. It might be, as it was at one school, that only a single person 'liked' the anonymous Facebook page, set up to spread rumours about Year 9 students. 'The teachers knew who it was immediately. I mean, who would "like" the account they set up?' Meredith says. Nicole's friend was on the receiving end of a police investigation. 'My friend made a fake account and the person she was taking off spotted it, and then the police and her parents got involved.' The police also got involved in Naomi's case, after she started receiving online threats. The culprit, police found, was a paedophile.

And as harrowing as all of this is, targeted girls admit that they rarely tell their parents they've become a victim. They will feel wretched. Their marks might plummet. They will cry themselves to sleep. But many of these teens will not walk out to the lounge room and confide in their parents. Why? Because what's worse than the abuse is the thought that their mobile phone will be confiscated on the grounds of safety. That was Kellie's fear. As she sat on the floor, wanting to shut the world out, she knew her parents' response would be to take her phone away so that she couldn't be hurt any further. That meant, in her mind, she couldn't tell them. Eventually, though, a family friend stepped in and convinced her to call a male friend who others in the group saw as a leader. She did, and he convinced her friends that she couldn't have possibly uploaded the savage posts while on a wifi-free holiday. One by one, her friends returned, and the tears stopped and the smiles came back. Eventually, the culprit outed herself: she and Kellie shared a biology class. They'd never talked, or even met, but Kellie had been easy prey. 'Who knows why someone does it?' Kellie says now. 'Perhaps they're jealous. Perhaps they're just bored.'

School-based youth health nurse Helene Hardy agrees with the boredom comment. With more than 13 years' experience in child and adolescent mental health, Hardy says girl groups routinely target someone, often out of tedium. 'Sometimes it's the old survival of the fittest. I've seen it over and over.' And while it happened when we were all at school, a crucial difference defines 2017. 'Home was an escape. But that's not the case anymore with these kids,' she says. She tells them to ignore the abuse. 'Don't respond. Don't get caught in that cycle of escalation. Block.' They are incredulous at that last piece of advice. Block? Turn their phone off? 'Even though they are being bullied [...] it's almost as though they're not sure they'd even be allowed to do that. [Their phone is] their life. I tell them that's their time, at home, away from all those worries.' The problem, as Hardy explains, is that an increasing number of working parents, and busy lives, result in girls being alone more at home. 'So they rely on that social media as their contact with the outside world.'

Switched on

Our teens now live in an online world. Sometimes foreign to those of us who still treasure receiving a written birthday card, it's the way they explore, read, play, learn and communicate. The average age for a child to own a smartphone is now 10.3 years and between the ages of 10 and 12 years almost 40 per cent of children boast at least one social media account.[1] These are the official figures, but ask an expert and those numbers start to sound very conservative. Cyber safety expert Susan McLean, for example, says she believes more than 70 per cent of children in Years 3 and 4 are using one or more age-restricted social networking sites. McLean visits schools regularly to talk about online dangers. Of one recent school visit she says, '123 out of 140 Year 5 students were using one or more age-restricted social networking sites.' That's close to 88 per cent of children in that peer group.

McLean became a police officer in Victoria in 1982 and a couple of years later joined the police community involvement program, which placed police officers in schools. She remembers a Year 8 coordinator at one school contacting her and asking for someone to attend the school to speak to students. The coordinator wanted 'the police talk'. It was 1994, and Susan didn't own a mobile phone. Two girls had had an argument and the offender had visited an adult sex chat room and posted an ad: 'If you want free sex, please contact this girl'. She included the name, address and phone number of the classmate she didn't like. 'She could not have foreseen the consequences for the victim and the family. A stream of men came knocking on the door looking for the 13-year-old girl with her very kind offer of free sex. The family had to temporarily move to a motel, and I had my cyberbullying baptism by fire,' McLean says.

Back in 1994, cyber harrassment was less widespread, partly because of the limited availability of devices and platforms. Now, at 14, the most popular social media sites are Instagram, Snapchat, Facebook, Kik, Skype, YouTube, Pinterest and Tumblr, but Twitter, Line, Kakao Talk and ooVoo also feature, amongst others. Of the 192 teen girls I questioned, almost all had several of them. In the main, their parents were aware they were on social media – but were not aware of the specific details. But here's a twist: it's often the good girl – the well-behaved class leader who is unaware of the detention room, who finds herself in trouble. McLean, who also authored *Sexts, Texts & Selfies*, says she has learnt that it's usually the child deemed least susceptible who can end up in trouble, making it difficult for both teachers and parents to understand. Teachers agree, making the point that nothing prohibits an A-student from being drawn to social media – despite being well-mannered, good at making decisions and a pleasure to teach. McLean remembers one incident in New South Wales where a teen rented a dodgy room in the Sydney CBD to meet men she'd contacted through social media. 'The parents said to me that she'd never put a foot wrong. She was a good kid.' Another, two years short of 14, begged her mother for an Instagram account. The captain of her primary school, her mother relented, despite it not being legal to have an account before the age of 13. 'Between Christmas and getting Instagram and the start of school, she'd stripped naked and sent photos to someone who had promised her a TV appearance.'

This is frightening because we don't expect our good girls, with clear decision-making skills, to get into serious trouble. But listen to teachers and school nurses and police officers and, more often than not, high achievers are being nabbed, constantly, for social media–inspired naughtiness. 'I can tell you, it's across the board,' one school principal told me. 'It's not public or private schools. In fact, it more often misses the average kids. That's why I say I'm really, really happy to have average kids.'

One school nurse tells the story of a beautiful Year 12 school leader whom she found bawling her eyes out. 'She'd sent a photo of herself to someone when she was 14, and her friends back then were now using it against her. '"My parents don't know about it. Now I'm worried it's going to turn up again. What do I do?" she asked me.' The nurse advised her to tell her mother about it. The girl did, and her panic subsided.

To those of us brought up in the 1980s, or even the 1990s, the idea of stripping off, taking a photograph and then sending it to someone seems risible. That's perhaps why I find the most shocking social media revelation while researching this book to be the number of 14-year-olds who had taken their clothes off, at least to their waist, and forwarded on the photograph. Mostly the addressee was a girlfriend, with a harmless caption like 'I'm growing boobs'. Often, it was also sent to a boy who had asked, and whom Miss 14 really liked. Of course, he promises not to pass it on. 'I never thought he'd do anything with it. He said it was private,' one 14-year-old told me. The extent of this, as a problem, only really came to a general understanding last year, with revelations that 70 Australian schools were being targeted by a pornography ring, hosted on a server on the other side of the world. That night, so many of us sat our girls down and told them that those naked photos would now travel the globe forever; the young girls who had sent them to someone, believing they would not be shared, would pay the price for years.

Alex Curtis, Counselling Centre Supervisor at Kids Helpline, says calls from 14-year-olds who had sent a topless photograph to someone were regular. 'We'll get a young girl call who is really distressed. She's taken a photo and sent it to a guy who says, of course, that it's all private. The next minute it's gone out and they have no idea how to then manage it. Often there's the threat that if they tell anyone, they'll send a copy to the mum and dad,' she says. On many occasions, it's not sent to a friend or a male they are trying to impress. Sometimes your 14-year-old is just wanting attention, and is lured in by sites who prey on teens. 'It can be a way of them getting attention and having someone say, "You're beautiful", "You're this and you're that,"' Curtis says.

Jon Rouse, one of Australia's leading paedophile investigators, shrugs when I suggest my research would indicate that about one-third of teen girls had sent a half-naked photograph of themselves to someone else. That didn't surprise him – although he thought the real figure might be higher. He points outside his inner-city Brisbane office, where national Task Force Argos is based. 'Out there in victim identification, our guys are arresting offenders who horde those images. They circulate on the net. There are collectors of those pictures of kids.' McLean agrees, saying anecdotally she believes the percentage of 14-year-olds who send a half-naked picture to someone else could even be as high as 80 per cent. Often the naked or topless girl will crop her own head out of the photo before sending it, falsely believing she is no longer

identifiable. 'That's what I see in the schools I visit ...
from the middle of nowhere to the top, most prestigious
girls' schools in every state and territory in Australia, and
I'm in the local government high school that has 95 per
cent of kids from overseas – and it really doesn't change,'
McLean says. These images are rarely sent via Instagram
or Facebook because of the controls that operate; the
usual transmission method is by text or by Snapchat,
where they falsely believe they can control how long the
image remains on show.

I put the figure of one in three to the principal of a big
girls' school. She nodded slowly. 'That's realistic.' She told
of one school, last year, that suspended several girls after
they photographed themselves naked at a party and sent
the images to each other. Before long, the photographs
were popping up everywhere, and the school found itself
trawling through 300 images. 'The idea of standing in
front of a mirror and taking a selfie when you are naked
and then sending it to a friend ...' The principal shook
her head. 'Then they'll turn and say, "But I only sent it
to a friend, I did nothing wrong!" and then some of the
parents will claim the same thing.' Another principal,
in another state, says parents need to step up and take
some responsibility. 'We talk about about social media,
we write about it, we arrange for speakers to come – and
then nobody will turn up – and then you have parents
saying, "We need to do something about this."' A lot of

the bad behaviour on social media happens at home, and parents are responsible there, that principal says. Another issue is that schools struggle to keep up with educating girls about technology. Often their first mistake comes before they understand all the safety tips available to them. In primary school, the focus is on cyber safety rather than on their digital footprint and sexting. That means they are arriving in high school without a wider understanding of what can go wrong and how they should protect themselves.

The regularity with which girls send these photographs stumped me. What could possibly be the rationale? 'They don't understand the consequences of it,' Rouse says. 'They're not thinking beyond the next five minutes. It's cool. It's kind of sexy. They're all exploring their sexuality. They're thinking, "All of my friends are doing it" or "He might like me a bit more if I do it" – it's all of those teenage hormone things that are going on. They are not thinking that when [they're] 18 or 19, that picture is still going to be floating around on the internet – and it is.' When asked the same question, McLean nominates three reasons quickly: girls are badgered or pressured into it; they are in a relationship or trying to attract someone's attention; or they are being groomed by a predator. The biggest, she says, is pressure. 'It's, "I expect you to share naked photos with me and if you don't you're going to be a nun. Or frigid."' School leaders see boys, usually, as the instigator here. This does not excuse the girls, because they are acquiescing and sending on the photographs. But boys are demanding it, meaning the education being delivered to girls needs to be widened to tell teen boys that they must not ask for photos.

It will be a few years down the track, when our daughters are trying to snare a university place or the job of their dreams, that the photographs are likely to come back to haunt them. In fact, in the past year Rouse points to a steady increase in requests from teenagers aged 18 to 20, and their parents, to remove images from the internet. 'They're saying, "This picture of me is on this site in China." We're like, "What do you want us to do about that? You did it. You sent it."' But at 14, it's hard to see past the next text. Or the boy who wants the photograph, ahead of the next dance.

The criminal ramifications here should not be overlooked. A 14-year-old girl who takes a half-naked photograph of herself is conceivably producing child exploitation material, and then distributing it. Her friend, the receiver, is in possession of it. That means both of them, potentially, are in trouble. 'But would we prosecute?' Rouse is asking the rhetorical question. 'No. That's not what we're here to do. But if he [the receiver] then sends it on to his mates, we would start looking at that with a degree of concern.'

Beware

Of course, you only read about the really bad scandals, and Rouse has a pocketful of them. The 14-year-old who met a guy online. She thought it was kind of cool that this older guy was interested in her, and eventually agreed to meet him. 'She turned up and he pulled her into his car and attempted to digitally penetrate her,' says Rouse. 'She managed to break free and run.' But the scary thing here is that she didn't tell anyone immediately. And the man continued to harass her. 'Every time she'd hop online he would immediately hit her up on instant messaging. She had no idea what to do.' Ultimately she told her mother, who contacted Task Force Argos. 'We asked her a few questions and then she divulged the other accounts she held that her mother didn't know about.' Officers from Task Force Argos took over her persona, logged on, agreed to meet the man, and promptly arrested him. He was in his early 20s.

Last year, a 13-year-old was befriended by a person she believed to be a 12-year-old girl. As they became friendly, the questions started. Have you ever had sex? What are you doing? Wearing? Those questions amount to what experts call 'grooming'. 'Don't tell anybody,' the alleged 12-year-old would say, 'this is our secret.' They started sharing images of each other. Two girls, talking to each other – or so the 13-year-old thought. Then one day her mother looked at her social media account and saw the conversation. Startled, she contacted Task Force Argos. The 12-year-old turned out to be a 35-year-old man.

In another case, police are investigating a father who has created fake social media accounts making out he's a good-looking male teenager. 'All these girls – his daughter and her friends – have accepted his request on social media. They think they're talking to this really hot 17-year-old and they're not,' a police officer involved in the investigation says. 'It's the father of one of the girls. He's got 30 girls sending him all their correspondence, and he's joining in on it.' Here's the catch. That man, the father of a 14-year-old girl, is also a known paedophile.

Some of our girls will be caught up in those big cases that often make the news, but it's more likely to be the run-of-the-mill problem on social media that snares them. Shelley, the mother of a 14-year-old, says her daughter fell out with her group of close friends because she had simply 'liked' a comment made by someone else. 'She thought it was a joke. Then she was called up to the principal's office, and told that amounted to bullying. She was devastated, and didn't have the maturity to understand that it wasn't a joke. I told her if it was a joke, the barb would have been sent directly to the girl, not put on Facebook.' Her response? 'I never thought of that, Mum.' A friend of Shelley's understands exactly what she is saying. 'I keep trying to tell my daughter that texting is not like talking.'

That was prompted after her daughter jokingly texted her best friend with comments like, 'I hate you.' Her friend would respond with, 'Get stuffed.' A joke between friends. But here's the catch: you can't hear the smile in a voice or the intonation that shows words are butterflies, not bullets, and it can turn to custard quickly. 'I thought this girl – who is just like my daughter – could wake up in a different mood and not take it as a joke,' Shelley's friend said.

Senior Constable Kelly Humphries gives talks on sexting to 14-year-old girls, regularly. 'They don't realise it can go viral in minutes. It can be in Germany or on someone's Facebook account in England in a matter of minutes. Sally sends it on to ten people, ten people send it on to 100 people and their cousin in England. Then the whole world has it,' Humphries says. Her boss, Detective Senior Sergeant Grant Ralston says once a text is sent, it's impossible to take back. 'All you can do is educate them not to do it again. It's too late once it's out. You can't pull it back. You can't get to those thousands of people around the world. It's gone.'

Most teenagers are not aware of the legal ramifications of passing on material of an exploitative nature, or if they are, believe that they are not going to be tracked. Ralston, a father of boys, has told his sons of a case where a 14-year-old girl sent a topless picture of herself to her 16-year-old boyfriend. The boyfriend later left her for someone else – but kept the picture. 'It got a bit nasty and suddenly that person sent it to 20 mates and suddenly it got brought to school and shown to other younger students. And that opened another can of worms.' Not only was it an offence to post it online, but those people who were passing it on were further breaking the law by exposing younger people to it. 'It turned out to be 15–20 offenders in the end, because they were passing it on,' Ralston said. They could have all been charged with possession of child exploitation material, but instead the case was used as a formal warning to the teenagers in the hope that they would learn from it. Ralston says teenagers are doing it without knowing it is an offence. Both the person sending the photos and those passing it on were surprised they could be tracked. 'Everyone's got an IP address. Everyone's got a mobile number. It's all traceable. Even with fake accounts, there's usually an electronic or paper trail. I don't think 14-year-olds realise that.'

And that shouldn't be news to anyone. For years now, a steady trickle of stories has emerged of good young prospective employees being dropped because of something in their background. Employers routinely look at social media profiles before determining whether to give someone a job. But sometimes they can be scared off – not just by the conversation or the shenanigans they find online, but simply because of the number of 'friends' a person might have. Increasingly, it's not just talent or marks that are being prized, but perceptions of applicants, often gauged through social media. Their digital footprint, created for years, points to more than an email address. It includes photographs, friends, page likes, messages, content, blogs and even the tone of commentary.

How many people are following your 14-year-old?

A couple of years ago, Susan McLean was asked by some of our AFL clubs to prepare digital reputation reports on prospective AFL players. 'These were boys – talented footballers who were probably going to be drafted – but the clubs wanted to know what they were doing online,' she says. One potential player had 2900 friends listed on his Facebook account. 'So then I went in and went to the first six friends he had. I got their friends, added them together and divided by six to get an average and multiplied that by 2900, and the answer was 21 million.' That meant his postings could potentially be seen by 21 million people. Put yourself in the position of recruitment at an AFL club, keen not to court controversy or trouble down the track. It sends up a red alert. McLean says the exercise also serves as a warning to others, including 14-year-old girls. 'It's perception. It might be judgemental and it is harsh and it is unfair, but the reality is if someone can find it online they will use it either for you or against you, and you'd better hope it's not against you.' And if the AFL analogy doesn't fit, try this. If your child has 650 Facebook friends – a number McLean says is average – and they all have about 500 friends, that means 325 000 people could conceivably contact your child. 'The only word for that is dangerous,' she says.

But there's another dimension here, too, that experts urge parents to consider, and that's the nature of social media – one of the best tools for collaboration and communication. This is the girls' world, and because it can influence unduly it is crucial – as school principal after school principal told me – to teach early teens to filter the messages delivered and make up their own minds. Let's take Twitter as an example. Twitter is an online platform where users have 140 characters to say what they like. You sign up and follow who you like; and others can follow you. Some people have a dozen followers; others have millions. It's an efficient way to get daily news from whatever source you want, bite-sized pointers to interesting reads and access to celebrities and politicians and others who were impossible to access previously. But in 140 characters you need to be blunt. You don't have the luxury of explaining yourself – a point politicians have found repeatedly. The abuse and vitriol directly levelled at them (many of them author their own tweets) leave no doubt as to what voters might think of them individually. The nastiness has forced others to quit the social media platform, the judgements delivered into their inbox 24/7 making it too difficult to stay online. Google 'quit Twitter' and you'll find your own examples, but British actor and comedian Stephen Fry is a very public example. In February 2016 he deleted his account after a torrent of abuse in the wake of a joke he made at the British Academy Film and Television Arts awards.[2]

Social media influence

A terrific example of the influence of Twitter was shown in recent years by Microsoft programmers who created a chatbot (a program designed to simulate an intelligent conversation with human users) named Tay.[3] Tay was designed to talk and comment like a young person – a millennial. In that way, Tay would then learn how to interact more with people. That meant she'd be influenced by the conversation of those she was talking to, online. So what happened? It took 15 hours for the chatbot to be mirroring the racist and sexist comments of others. That's why the ability to filter messages, to proactively participate in conversations, or block commentary that isn't what you want, is so important. In another case, the British think tank Demos monitored the use of the words 'slut' and 'whore' over a three-week period by Twitter users based in Britain and found more than 6000 different users were targeted by 10 000 separate sexist tweets. Interestingly, half of all sexist tweets came from women.[4] That kind of environment is not confined to Twitter but it highlights starkly the online girls' world our 14-year-old daughters are trying to navigate.

Experts are split on which social media platforms can benefit teens, and which present the most difficulties, so it is understandable that parents are just as confused. Consider the answers – all by 14-year-old girls – to this question: what rules do your parents have in relation to your use of social media?

'I'm not allowed to use too much data.'

'Don't use it when you are with others. Only use it when you are alone.'

'Don't use social media at the table.'

'Don't use Instagram during meals.'

The list goes on, but you get the point. The most common rule related to the use of data and the financial consequences of that – not *how* and *when* the devices were being used. Of course there were exceptions to that:

'I hand my phone in every night. All accounts are checked.'

'If I fail [at school], I lose all social media.'

'Social media can only be used downstairs and I have to leave my phone downstairs when I go up to bed.'

'My parents trust me – but they shouldn't.'

The following hypothesis is put to the girls: it's 10.30 pm, and you're almost asleep. You hear the phone 'ding', meaning a message has just popped into one of your social media in-trays. What do you do? The response is a chorus: 'Check it!'

So what does punishment for a 14-year-old look like? It shouldn't be a surprise that taking away their smartphone is at the high end of hardship – and the one commonly used by parents. It might mean that hours are regained in a teen's day, but it also cuts them off from their friends, and often from their schoolwork. Indeed, it can force an isolation that runs much deeper than a simple home punishment. 'A lot of party invites go out through direct messaging and stuff,' Dani says. 'I find that some of my friends who aren't checking their friends or don't have it [because of punishment] get left out.' Dropped from a party list, or a planned after-school hot chocolate in the mall, or even a post-hockey catch-up takes on a life of its own. This is also the bugbear from the handful of Year 9 girls who have no social media. The reason they don't have social media accounts is twofold: either parents who believe it is dangerous or not needed; and others who have taken themselves off it because it took over their world. 'I used to be on it and I was addicted to it – so I'm not allowed at all now,' Katie says. And Anne says, 'I'm not on any. When I used it I got very addicted to it. I'd have to check it obsessively. Mum says I should be on it, but

I don't want to.' Even some with accounts are reluctant users. 'It just causes fights at our school,' one says. 'It causes a division of groups,' another says.

So what would happen if you had social media removed for a month? What would be the consequences? It's a scenario that few of them have even considered. Many of them say they'd cope. They'd get used to it. They'd find another way of catching up and talking to their friends. Others said it would mean they'd end up friendless. 'I would die,' several girls offered. But the big issue in turning off social media, for this cohort, is that they would lose their Snapchat streaks. Most girls are on several platforms, with Instagram and Snapchat winning out in the popularity stakes. But it's understandable, particularly given that many parents don't use the same platforms, that they struggle with deciding how many social media accounts their daughter should be permitted. But does that really matter? As one principal explained, it might just mean that each application chews up slightly less time as it shares its billing with others. Perhaps more pertinent is the question of whether their parents are aware of the number of different social media accounts they have. This time, the answers are equally divided – roughly half of their parents are in the loop. But those who said their parents were aware of their different social media applications were quick to add that Mum and Dad didn't really understand the difference between them. Even those girls whose parents followed them on social media said that their parents didn't really use the same social media – but wanted to be added to their 'friends' list.

How much do you understand?

This is a colossal issue. This world is not one that most parents understand. And even those who use Facebook to post their happy snaps and to keep in touch with friends, or Twitter to market their business, don't necessarily know the parameters around those platforms or many of the others. 'It's a mother's biggest concern when you talk to them,' says Nicky Kozlovskis, president of Mothers of Only Girls. 'It comes up time and time again – how do we handle it? I've asked the same question.' Nicky says many mothers are badgered by their daughters to be allowed onto Instagram before they turn 13, because all of their friends are already on it. And then it's Facebook, and then Snapchat. Ask most mums directly what they understand of these sites, and their answers show where the problem might lie.

'I don't understand any of it.'

'They are so much more advanced than we are with technology, even before 14.'

'I try and keep up and then you hear these horror stories about predators and girls sending photos.'

Many of those photos, their mothers say, are 'innocent in themselves'.

'It might be a bikini shot, and as a mother I'm horrified thinking that every predator is looking at that – but she says it's only her friends. I just don't know. It's frightening and it keeps coming up [in our house].'

Perspective is important here. One teacher explains that at her school, most children can't afford a smart device, including a computer. Another mother, who works with a charity, says the chasm between what she deals with between 9 am and 5 pm, and what she does at home, is startling. 'One girl had an abortion at 13,' she says. In another case, a mother decided when she turned 40 that she didn't want to look after the children anymore, so made her 16-year-old daughter take over all responsibilities. 'Another had a mother who was paying her 14-year-old in cigarettes to clean the house,' she says. Perhaps many of these children also have a smart phone – and have to navigate these hardships as well as the hazards of social media.

It's worth keeping that in mind. Most children are privileged to be able to use social media as a means of communication and learning. It's the side problems that sometimes envelop those advantages – problems parents are not skilled in addressing – that are the issue.

Jon Rouse recently spoke at a school evening that included parents and came away shaking his head. He says that while the next generation will understand smart devices, the current crop of parents needs to step outside their comfort zones and learn how they work. 'They don't understand how the technology works because they don't use it themselves. They're not across the applications that are on their kids' phones. They don't even know how Snapchat works. Install it. It can be a good fun app – which is why kids use it.' Many other experts give different advice, but Rouse stands firm on his recommend-ation – and remember, he is the person who spends night and day running a team that attempts to identify those monsters who prey on our children. Rouse's point is this: social media apps can be used for good or bad; it's not the application but how it is used that presents a problem. Take, for example, television. Television brought news into our lounge rooms and allowed us to feel involved in the world's events. But too much television could be detrimental. The same applies with technology in Rouse's world. 'I know where my daughter is at any given time with Find My Friends,' he says. He produces his phone, fires it up and shows me a map. 'She's at my house,' he says. 'But are mums and dads aware that [the Find My Friends app] even exists on a phone?' The flip side of this is, are children sharing where they are with someone they shouldn't? 'Use Snapchat with a degree of caution,' says Rouse, 'don't think you're safe on it. Apps are not set up to cause grief, but [they] will as soon as they are not used with strict limitations.' Rouse says the security on Facebook is good, if you go through and set it up and understand it, and Instagram, likewise, is harmless and fun if used correctly. Rouse's view is supported by Associate Professor Alan Ralph from the Triple P Positive Parenting Program, which is headquartered in Brisbane and operates in 26 different countries. 'The bottom line is that parents need to help their kids to become intelligent consumers of the new technologies,' he says. 'Now you can't do that if you're not part of it, and so you're either leaving it to someone else or you're hoping that the kids will find it out without damage.' He says parental ignorance can be a boon to keeping the door open on communication, too: ask your daughter how to set up a social media account, and become involved. 'Use the technology. Instead of putting a note in the kids' lunchbox, text them,' Ralph says.

Of all the apps used by 14-year-olds, many experts agree that Kik is the most dangerous. Rouse says it is the application that most often comes to his attention as head of Task Force Argos. 'If I was going to take an app off my child, that's the one that I would,' he says. McLean agrees. 'Without a shadow of a doubt. No security. No blocking. No reporting. No way to stop random people contacting you. It's the number-one app for sexual predators worldwide.'

Helene Hardy says social media has a grip on 14-year-old girls irrespective of their friendship groups or upbringing. 'I have a rule that when they are with me they do not turn it on, and they even find that hard.' She sees that disconnect between teens and parents, daily. 'It's such a funny time. They don't know if they're Arthur or Martha. They think they should be connected to their parents but they're not. They're going through some stuff where they wish they had the connection. For me, that disconnection comes through so strongly. Parents go, "She's 14 now. What can I do? I've lost her." A lot of parents disconnect themselves from young people and they leave them to their own devices.'

Advice

Predators, according to Rouse, will look for open profiles that are easily accessible and where children will respond to messages. And he has this warning for parents: 'What we see is that kids will not tell their parents [if they get into trouble], out of embarrassment or fear that they will take the phone away from them. I wouldn't guess at the stats of kids who have come across something online – sent something by a potential predator or bullied badly by their friends – but who do not tell their parents about it.' He offers five pieces of advice for parents.

First, unless the communication channel is good and open, you will not find out what your 14-year-old is potentially confronting. 'It all comes back to the communication issue with Mum and Dad. Sit down with your kid. If you don't have an open, communicative relationship, you have no chance.' He doesn't pull any punches on the parent front. 'If you're not giving them the attention that they need because you're busy and too tired – which is our world – well, someone else is going to replace you.' Secondly, understand your child's social media profile. Share an account, or help them set it up. 'I'd say to them, "Let's google it, look at it, research the app and see what it can and can't do, and then install it and sit down together and know what it can do."' Thirdly, your child should not befriend online anyone they have not physically met in person. 'If you do not know this person in the real world, then you don't know who you are talking to. If they are not a friend in the real world, then they're not a friend. It's as simple as that.' Lucy, the parent of a 14-year-old, tells me how she was shocked to hear her daughter talking to someone, close to midnight. She had facetimed someone she had met online. But would that person have been welcomed into their home that late at night? Of course not, and that's Rouse's point. If you wouldn't allow it in the 'real' world, don't allow it online. Fourthly, if your

14-year-old comes and talks to you about something that has occurred online, believe her. Many parents, according to Rouse, are dismissive of the cyber concerns of their children, when his anecdotal evidence would suggest that 90 per cent of them are telling the truth. 'If they've taken the time to tell you something, please listen.' His plea is corroborated by other experts. At one rural school earlier this year, McLean had 12 children make disclosures after her session that required action by the school or police. 'There's a real deficiency in kids being prepared to come forward, and I don't know why,' McLean says. 'What bothers me is, had I not visited the school, nobody would know about these kids.' McLean says the level to which girls are willing to put up with 'stuff' without telling an adult is alarming. 'They appear to have a tolerance level for online abuse in particular. I often get asked, "How much abuse should I tolerate before I tell someone?" If a girl will tolerate online abuse she's more likely to tolerate sexual abuse and physical abuse and psychological abuse.' And don't believe that Rouse and his team can't track down the perpetrators. Many times parents believe the culprits are overseas and don't report it. Jon Rouse spends his days and nights investigating them, and will take up cases brought to police attention.

Fifth and finally, according to Rouse, don't confiscate your daughter's mobile phone as a punishment. 'Taking the phone off them is not the answer because they can log in on any number of other devices,' he says. 'You make them a social leper and you're not doing a very good job of keeping an open communication with your child by doing that.'

There's one other factor here. Some 14-year-olds are sending more than 100 texts each night, and about 45 per cent of teens aged 14 to 16 regularly send texts after 3 am. So, as you nod off to sleep in the bedroom next door, do you know, for sure, what your daughter is doing?

The sleep nightmare

'1 am. 2 am.
I just stay up 'cause I'm not tired.'

TIFFANY,
14

Let me introduce you to four 14-year-old girls: Mandy, Margaret, Joanne and Liz. They could be your daughters or nieces or neighbours, given how common their stories are. All four bring home strong report cards; three of them play sport and the other spends hours each week, late into the night, at ballet class. All four of them are drunk tired.

'We go from school to sport to homework to bed to sport, back to school. And then you have to fit part-time work and friends in there. It's too hard.' – MANDY

'A good night is five hours for me. A bad one can be three hours.' - MARGARET

'It's so hard to get out of bed of a morning. And if I have two consecutive nights' sleep of only six or seven hours, on that third day I can't cope. And then Mum will just say something and I'll go off.' - JOANNE

'I can have devices in my room so I get distracted and it gets later and later. Sometimes I wish my parents would enforce that rule of no devices in the bedroom, but I'm not going to suggest it. That would be stupid.' - LIZ

Today, school is only part of a hectic teen's day, and for many 14-year-old girls, the day can reach far into the night. Rowing can start before the moon nods off to sleep, meaning an alarm clock cuts through any teen dreams as early as 4.15 am. Rowing morphs into school, which becomes hockey or swimming training or netball practice. Home beckons, but means a quick shower and dinner. And the clock chimes 8.30 pm. Often, this is when many girls first open their books to begin the assigned homework. Study and revision has to wait.

Mandy, Margaret, Joanne and Liz are not exceptions to the rule; that's the issue here. Busy-bee lives are unfolding each day in high schools across Australia, and the impact is devastating. Teachers report yawns from 9 am, and brain experts say learning while tired is pretty much useless.

Parents admit they're not sure what time their teens nod off, and many girls nominate a lack of sleep as the key reason behind conflict with their parents. 'If I'm really tired I'll just yell at everyone and everything,' Pippa says.

Heavy school workloads, on top of extracurricular activities, are a key reason behind an epidemic in sleep deficit. Our 14-year-olds are worried sick, even if they are not telling you. It might be anxiety over an upcoming test, or friendship angst that follows her home from school. The lure of the blue-lit screen resting on the bedside table adds to the problem, with the short-wavelength light emitted suppressing the sleep hormone and delaying sleep onset. In lay terms, the teen's brain is being told it's time to wake up. And then, when they wake to a piercing alarm the next morning, what is their first act? That question is put to a group of Brisbane 14-year-olds. The answer is so in tune it seems practised: 'Check my phone.'

Sarah goes to bed between 10.30 pm and 11.30 pm. 'Maybe 12.30 am if I have a big workload. I would love to go to bed at 10 pm though.' Pressed, Sarah admits she is on Instagram, Tumblr, Snapchat, Facebook, Twitter, Skype and ooVoo. Sheepishly, she also owns up to the fact that she's only allowed social media between 4 pm and 9.30 pm – so doesn't begin her homework until 9.30 pm. Her case points to another issue: few 14-year-olds have curfews, and those who do largely ignore them, tucked in their room with the door closed, while their parents, tired themselves, nod off to sleep up the corridor.

When this picture is described to Dr Chris Seton at the Woolcock Institute of Medical Research, he nods his understanding. None of this is a surprise. Also a paediatric and adolescent sleep physician at Westmead Children's Hospital, Dr Seton hears it every day. About 80 per cent of his patients are drawn from private schools, many of them weighed down by nonstop extracurricular activity cycles and hours of homework. Seven in every ten 14-year-old girls gets insufficient sleep, most of them recording fewer than eight hours, when nine hours is the minimum required. About 15 per cent, Seton says, sleep for only five hours each night. Seton's passion for the challenge shows itself in the frustration he holds over the sleep-deficit epidemic that is still not accepted as a public health issue. Teenagers are using stimulants to stay awake, just to finish assigned homework, and some private schools pay no heed to the size of workloads given to teens. The average 14-year-old with 30 minutes of missed sleep records a measurable IQ difference of up to 10 points, he says. Ten points! Isn't that enough information for this to be treated as a serious public health issue? Mild sleep apnoea equated to losing two grades in terms of learning – an A becomes a C; a B becomes a D. Why wouldn't that hard evidence win parents over? And it doesn't stop there. Seton says a string of other links – between insufficient sleep and drug and alcohol use, depression and anxiety – also exists, and the problem continues to grow.

The drop in academic results recorded by tired students can be explained by how sleep loss affects short- and long-term memory; the old adage 'in one ear and out the other' is truer than we might have believed. Short-term memory loss can happen with one night's missed sleep. For good long-term memory, a teen needs sufficient sleep to consolidate their learning. 'Say a child gets a good night's sleep and they're in the classroom and they're learning well on that particular day and accomplishing short-term memory,' Seton says, 'that learning only goes to long-term memory if they have consolidated sleep the night after. So Rapid Eye Movement (REM) sleep consolidates learning. If they get a good night and they learn well during the day and then they sleep badly [the next] night, the memory has not gone into long-term memory.'

But it's not just a matter of introducing a curfew and sending your 14-year-old off to bed, whether her home-work is complete or not. Earlier bedtimes are impractical for teens, whose body clocks make it searingly hard to fall asleep early, as I will explain shortly. What *would* work best, according to experts the length and breadth of the globe, is to encourage society to fit in with teenagers. That would mean allowing them to stay up late, recognising that it is almost impossible for them to fall asleep early and that 15 per cent – or one in six teens – have difficulty sleeping, no matter what. That cohort, with or without technology and pressure, still struggled to nod off at any time, even during school holidays.

While it hasn't seeped through public policy in any real sense in Australia, sleep is increasingly seen as the third pillar of good health in many countries, alongside diet and exercise, and research demonstrating that adolescent sleep deprivation has links not only to drug and alcohol use, but also to traffic accidents, could be the alarm needed here. In fact, it was a grant by the United States–based Centers for Disease Control and Prevention in Atlanta that threw up stunning results that have prompted many schools, worldwide, to have the debate over whether they should delay their opening hours. The piece of research was a three-year study involving 9000 students, aged between 14 and 18.[1] The students attended one of eight public high schools in three US states – Minnesota, Colorado and Wyoming. Dr Kyla Wahlstrom, the lead author on the 2014 report, says that while social and environmental factors partially explained late sleep times, the sleep–wake cycle of teens had identified changes in specific biological processes that occurred with the onset of puberty, which meant teenagers not only needed more sleep but also felt sleepy at a later time. 'They all fall asleep pretty much around a quarter to eleven or 11 pm, and their brains don't really wake up until eight in the morning,' she says.

'The human [teen] body is seeking about nine or nine-and-a-quarter hours' sleep every night.'

Wahlstrom and her research team looked at whether or not a delay of more than an hour in the start time for high school students had an impact on students, specifically on their health or their academic performance. Survey data was drawn from the 9000 students, who were individually questioned about their daily activities, substance use and sleep habits. The team also used students' academic reports – grades, attendance, punctuality and how they fared on state and national tests – as part of the investigation. And what did they find? 'Later start times had a statistically significant positive impact on grades,' Wahlstrom says. 'It's very powerful data.' In Jackson Hole, Wyoming, for example, a statistically significant improvement was recorded in all subjects – English, Maths, Social Studies and Science, and in all grades. Every subject. Every year level. Parents' reactions were also tested as part of the survey, and perhaps it's less surprising to parents of 14-year-olds that 92 per cent believed their children were easier to live with when school started later in the morning.

While research has looked at the link between academic performance and sleep for many years, perhaps the most interesting part of this research related to its focus on car accidents. In the United States, students are able to drive at 16 years of age. A comparison was drawn between teens driving to school for an early start – 7.30 am – compared with a school start closer to 9 am. 'When the high schools started later [...] we had a 70 per cent reduction in car crashes,' Wahlstrom says. 'It's phenomenal.' I think I have heard her wrong. Seventeen per cent? No, she says. Seventy per cent. The data is gold for public policy experts, particularly when looked at in the context of science – eye blink rates, the speed with which teen drivers can brake, how much attention they pay to their peripheral vision, and their inexperience. 'Schools and public policy officials need to be thinking about teen drivers – not only as a public safety to themselves, but they could be crashing into us,' Wahlstrom says. 'This has to be something that can't just be attributed to lazy teens or teens that are totally distracted because they're doing something on their iPhones or something like that.'

Wahlstrom's findings are mentioned to me repeatedly by others during the research for this book. The staggering figure of a 70 per cent reduction in car crashes is raised again and again. What other evidence do we need to reconsider the scheduling around our teenagers? 'When they have a late body clock, getting them up at 7 am is like you and me getting up at 3 am,' Seton says. Neural and systems complexity specialist Dr Fiona Kerr, from the University of Adelaide, points to the two times in our lives that our brains undergo major reshaping. One is as a baby, the other is as a teenager around puberty. Sleep deprivation could alter brain development, she says, particularly the frontal lobe, which is critical for logic and reasoning skills.

The list of problems associated with drowsy teenagers runs to pages. Impaired learning. Mood swings. Anxiety. Depression. More prone to developing a negative body image. Low self-esteem. A loss of their sense of humour. Sleep-hungry teens are also more likely to eat fast food two or more times a week, have difficult relationships with their parents, increase school absenteeism and be put on detention. 'Not getting enough sleep causes the number of T cells in a teenager's body to fall by 30 to 40 per cent, thereby reducing the ability of their immune system to fight everyday infections,' Seton adds. They are also more likely to suffer headaches than their peers who are not sleep deprived. Additional research is also finding that half of those kept awake by electronic devices suffered from a wide variety of mood and cognitive problems, including ADHD.

With that knowledge, it's not surprising that Kids Helpline often receives calls from high school students late into the night. Many of them are studying, and anxious, or still on their phones. But, despite the enormous amount of money poured into the education system and the focus on how best to test our students, nothing has changed to assist their sleep patterns. And it's not just experts, academics, the medical profession and teenagers themselves pleading for a probe into when the day starts and ends. Teachers, principals and school nurses also see the impact of tired teens daily.

'I've talked to Year 9s – and they are up until 1 am and 1.30 am on a weekday, and most of the time their parents don't know. They [the parents] have relinquished the whole [no] device thing in the room. And I've seen the result working in mental health units where cyberbullying has gone to such an extreme where these kids have tried to commit suicide because they've felt so alone. That's a sad reality.' – A SCHOOL NURSE

'I make my own child (aged 12) go to bed at 7.30 pm even if she can't sleep because I see what it does to girls every day. I don't think they realise how sleep deprivation affects them. And it's accumulative, too.' – SOPHIE, A TEACHER OF 14-YEAR-OLD GIRLS

'All the science tells us we should be starting later. The biggest issue, of course, is that schools also play a major role in childcare, and while the workplace doesn't mirror school life I think it is unlikely that it will happen.' – JANE, A SCHOOL PRINCIPAL

So significant is the problem that some schools have instituted 'sleep hygiene lessons' as part of life-skills programs, where students are taught a routine to get ready for bed. That's right: in Year 9! Seton is teaching the same routine in his clinics. Forty-five minutes before bed, all technology is turned off, then the teen has a bath. A chilled music playlist is turned on, a snack and a drink devoured, before the teen slips into bed. 'It trains the brain to get ready for sleep,' Seton says. 'It means when the light goes off the brain is not racing. Their mood is better.' But few follow it. Indeed, in the dozens and dozens of adolescents queried as part of this project, none could define what 'sleep hygiene' might mean. 'The kids I am seeing are often in crisis,' Seton says. Increasingly, 14-year-old students who attend his clinic are being asked by the school to show cause for absenteeism – all caused, he believes, by a lack of sleep.

Of course, social media plays a significant role here, and while it has been dealt with elsewhere in this book, experts say twin challenges faced most teenagers: relinquishing their phone at night; and rising early in the morning. Phones are routinely taken into their bedrooms, sometimes even left under the pillow, when sleep finally takes hold. But each time a message pops in, and the phone dings, the seduction to pick it up wins out. And if it's not the welcome noise of a friend's message, it's the comfort of the blue light feeding the urge to stay up and chat for just a little bit longer. Teenage girls in particular, say experts, suffer FOMO (fear of missing out) if they turn their device off overnight. (It might be that crucial message from a friend, an invitation to the school dance, a piece of gossip they can't live without.) They'd rather suffer tiredness than arrive at school, into their peer group, being the only one who wasn't up with the nocturnal electronic goings-on. That is borne out in the data showing the percentage of teens texting – not just after midnight but after 3 am on weeknights. Put plainly, it's unnerving. Seton says about 45 per cent of teens aged 14 to 16 regularly sent texts after 3 am, and 75 per cent after midnight. Some were sending more than 100 texts a night. The average sat at 34. 'That data is irrefutable,' he says. 'It's based on phone records.' It's not only sending the texts that's part of the equation; the anticipation of waiting for a reply to a text means the brain wakes up – a term called 'infomania'. The claim by teens that their phone is needed for its alarm can quickly be eliminated by buying an alarm clock.

If modelling is crucial for our offspring to determine what is important, we are not setting the best example ourselves. Think of the last time, as a parent, you had a full night's sleep. Usually something gets in the way: a good book, a late movie, an extra glass of wine, a sick child, a big project. The list goes on. The same goes for many jobs. Once, while working on ABC radio, I was encouraged to undertake a 'sleep experiment'. It meant that I would not sleep, but broadcast twice, in a 30-hour time period. The rationale for the experiment was to question how our junior doctors, rostered to work 24 hours or more, could possibly do their job well. How could they focus on a diagnosis? How could they be alert enough to make a quick decision in the accident and emergency department? I spoke to many doctors who revealed how they snatched a nap on a chair between pager calls, and how they often felt they didn't quite do as good a job as they had hoped. One chilling fact will remain with me forever. Some doctors didn't even remember driving home at the end of their shift. They remembered signing off and climbing into their cars, but not the journey snaking through city and suburban streets to home. That's nightmarish on the medical front, but also points to a significant potential problem on our roads. Of course, I didn't have the life-and-death decisions that go with intensive care. I didn't have to grab a packet of salty chips from a vending machine for dinner, or be shaken every 10 minutes with a call to make a necessary or life-or-death decision. Nor did I have to practise not going to the toilet, as one doctor told me, until my bladder was about to burst. But I stayed awake from 4 am one day until midday the next day. After 16 or 20 hours I felt furry. A bit slurry perhaps. And then a little bit drunk, although nothing and no-one were funny. The sense of tiredness actually passed, but my ability to act quickly, to think clearly and to navigate an issue was impaired.

Curiously, we still take pride in announcing to our Facebook friends that we stayed up until midnight cooking, or that we crammed an 'all-nighter' to finish a big project, or that the dinner party was so good it lasted until 3 am. So with us sending that message, it's difficult, perhaps, to turn to our teens and negotiate a night's sleep that tallies to nine hours.

Andrew May, a partner in the KPMG performance clinic, says productivity and health suffer through sleep deprivation. He quotes one study finding that only sleeping six hours a night for 12 days straight is the same as being awake for a full 24 hours. 'And the cognitive and physical performance of someone who's been awake for 24 hours is similar to a person with a blood alcohol reading of 0.1,' May says. 'The impact of sleep deprivation affects everything from attention and concentration to emotional reactions, problem-solving skills, and even moral judgement.' Six years ago, he says, Harvard scientists suggested that a lack of sleep cost US companies US$63.2 billion in lost productivity per year.

In the search for solutions for teenagers, experts raise their vanity as a possible smart means of prompting them to take personal ownership of their sleep. That means equating sleep with looking better, having clear skin and shiny hair, feeling better, doing better at school and living longer. Research shows all that to be true, too. The idea behind this approach is that it gives a 14-year-old girl, under pressure to stay connected, the impetus and the confidence to claim back time, to tell her friends that she is not going to answer texts in the middle of the night because she is sleeping. To do that would turn down the controls on the social pressure dial that dictates that each and every text needs to be read and acknowledged.

Hopefully, the pride badges we wear for living on little sleep are also becoming a little bit worn. That's certainly the aspiration in the slow move by companies to reward the company's best sleepers rather than those who stay on at their desk until after midnight. Andrew May says expectations to meet deadlines, compounded with other factors like travel, social obligations and family, meant sleep was usually the first thing to go. 'I've heard executives boast about how little time they snooze. It's become a competition. If only they knew how much they were shortchanging their performance,' he says. He gives the example of Aetna, a United States–managed health-care company, which is leading the march in the opposite direction. Here CEO Mark Bertolini has declared that workers who sleep well could provide a boost to business.[2] Putting his money where his mouth is, workers who can prove they sleep for seven hours or more a night for 20 consecutive days receive a bonus of $25 a day (up to $500 a year). Fitness trackers are used to help workers, who are also provided with sleep information and yoga and meditation skills.

Arianna Huffington, founder and former editor-in-chief of the *Huffington Post*, has also brought a bit of welcome celebrity to the call for more sleep. Author of several books, including *The Sleep Revolution* and *Thrive*, Huffington's campaign follows her own episode, in 2007, when she collapsed from exhaustion. It was a personal wake-up call. Huffington says sleep needs to become a priority for everyone. Just pop *why am* into Google, she says, and before you can type the next word its auto function will complete it for you: *why am I so tired* pops up first, closely followed by *why am I always tired*. Speaking at the 2016 National Coalition of Girls' Schools conference in New York, she received a rock-star's welcome for her call for us to redefine, as part of that re-prioritising, what success means. The audience – educators in girls' schools the world over – saw, on a daily basis, the devastating impact that a sleepless night waged on a student. 'We need to educate our young girls that they don't have to burn out to succeed,' Huffington told the packed room. School start times needed to be changed, too, she said; they made no sense currently.

That latter comment – about school start times – is almost universally supported – by students, teachers, doctors, psychologists, brain experts and academics. Wahlstrom, who is also a former school administrator and school principal, knows the hurdles such a suggestion raises: it interferes with child minding; it disrupts peak hour; the logistics don't work; the list goes on. 'But the community has to come together,' she says. 'The thing the community needs to do is have a discussion with the facts at hand.' That means the community needs to look at the link between drowsy teens and the recorded links with drug use, car crashes, academic results, alcohol use, depression and a long list of other issues. Still to this day in the United States, hundreds of thousands of teenagers are being awoken at 6 am to start their first class at 7.15 am. In Australia, change has been slow, but at least it's edging in the right direction. Since the effect of teen sleep patterns was first studied decades ago, public policy officials have been coming to the table, and some schools are at least trialling later starting times.

The perfect time for high school gates to swing open is a matter for debate, but if an ideal night's sleep for teens runs from 10.45 pm until 8 am, school should not begin before 9 am, Wahlstrom says. That would allow a 14-year-old to rise, get ready and travel to school. School programming could then run later, because it was the starting time, not the length of the day, that was at issue. Dr Seton agrees. Society needed to accommodate the needs of teens because there were so many of them, and sleep deprivation was causing crises, he says. 'And the big part of society that needs to accommodate them is schools,' he says. Seton says a 10 am or a 10.30 am start time would be the best-case scenario.

But here in Australia, few are onboard, in practice. In theory, educators applaud the idea. They want their teen classes awake and engaged. They see the problem brought on by lack of sleep and drowsiness. It plays out in class, and again at lunchtime. But it's not as easy as it looks. Certainly some Australian schools have been tinkering with start times, but there is no mass move to allow high school students to begin their daily education a bit later. Some schools have raised it as an option, but support for it amongst families is low. And in some cases, there has been strong opposition to trialling later start times. Jane Danvers, principal of the Wilderness School in South Australia, like most of her peers, agrees with the science behind calls to change the school day. But she says obstacles exist to make it difficult and schools frequently looked at other ways to cater for teens. For example, timetables were often structured to differentiate what was taught in morning classes and what was taught in afternoon classes.

At the moment, the 8.30 am to 3 pm model slips into bus and train timetables, allows homework to be done before dinner, and doesn't create a logistical problem for big cities. In other words, it's neat. It's clean. It works, for almost everyone. The one demographic missing out here are the teens – where the 14-year-old girls sit smack bang in the middle.

Pocket money, please

'If Mum and Dad are on the right track financially, you will be as well. But the opposite is also true.'

ANDREA CINCOTTA,
secondary school teacher and financial literacy expert

On the day Amelia turned 14 years and nine months, she started job-hunting. Some of her school friends had snagged after-school or weekend employment and they seemed loaded with cash. They'd splurged on new make-up, including a 'totes amazeballs' shimmer powder, and concert tickets. One had even bought a Mimco purse. Amelia's parents gave her $10 a week, some weeks. Other weeks they'd forget about pocket money, and when she'd remind them they'd tell her to look for a part-time job. It would be good for her, they'd say. It would teach her about service, and the value of money. 'I didn't care where I got a job, I just wanted one really badly. I'd do anything,' Amelia says.

The job hunt, at the age of 15, for Amelia's mother or father 30 years ago would have been so much easier. A friend of a friend would have helped out by offering menial work after school in their local business. Or the local supermarket would go on a hiring spree, wanting as many youngsters, on a junior wage, as possible. Or it might have been the local petrol station, or café, or the morning newspaper run where Amelia's parents found work. For me, it was in the clothes section of Coles in a town in rural Queensland. My bestie, Sue, worked alongside me, and each Saturday morning we'd curse the customers in footwear and lingerie.

Anyway, back to 2017. Amelia tried everywhere: fast food outlets that only wanted university students because of the shift work; big cafés that wanted university students because they were also licensed for evening opening hours; big retail chains which required online tests that her aunt and uncle, used to dealing with retailers, did for her – but she still didn't get called up. She tried bakeries, offering to do the before-school shift, ice-cream parlours, dress shops and cut-price chains, pharmacies and make-up shops, and any other outlet she could. The answer was the same wherever she applied: we don't want a résumé, or even to see you – just upload your details online and we'll be in touch if anything becomes available. That meant they couldn't see Amelia's private school uniform or her neatly tied-back hair, or even hear her manners. 'Look,' the licensee of one big ice-cream chain explained to her aunt, 'we know people send in the details but we're not going to look at them. If I need someone else, I'll just ask the best kid working for me whether they've got a friend who wants a job.'

Prominent national economist Saul Eslake had a part-time job picking strawberries as a teenager, and knows that job hunting in 2017 is a much harder task. Many unskilled job openings, such as mowing lawns, picking fruit, delivering newspapers and a host of others, had contracted due to changes in regulations, occupational health and safety laws, increases in minimum wages and automation. And while new job opportunities existed – computer coding work, or even small online businesses set up in their bedrooms – it seems only a lucky few are able to do that. That story – of a 14- or 15-year-old's job search – has been told to me over and over again, by teens and parents. In one case, a Year 12 school captain (who later was in the top 2 per cent in his state academically) applied for jobs for 18 months before giving up.

After-school or weekend job seekers represent one big cohort of teens. But there is another: a group who have been forbidden by their parents from taking any employ-ment because it might affect their studies. 'My parents say I've got to focus on school, not getting more money,' was a surprisingly common refrain from 14-year-olds. This group was headed by parents whose priority was their daughters' school grades. They believed that hours away from their children's desks meant vital revision would be missed and their marks therefore jeopardised. In some of those cases, parents even paid their children the equivalent of a part-time job – as long as they spent the time studying.

Several principals spoke out against that. Dr Amanda Bell, the principal of The Women's College within the University of Sydney, says that dissuading teens from real work did them no favours. Bell, a former school principal, has held leadership positions in both the public and private sectors across Australia. 'Paid work is just as important as the sporting team,' she says. If she was a school principal again, she would encourage parents to consider what their 14-year-old or 15-year-old might learn from paid work, particularly in retail and hospitality sectors. 'They'll learn how to cope with cross, cranky customers and not take it personally,' she says. 'They'll learn how to turn up regardless or they'll lose their job. There's no out for that. Jobs are competitive and you need to turn up. You'll have awful bosses who won't care – all those things . . .'

But back to pocket money. If the girls are homogenous, their pocket money is the polar opposite. Andrea Cincotta, a qualified secondary school teacher and a financial literacy expert, founded FIT – Financially Independent

Teenagers – and ran school workshops for students to understand money. One of the first questions she asked students was: do you receive money? And overwhelmingly they do. Of 600 Year 9 students (aged 14 and 15), 84 per cent of them told her they are given money. Usually that's in the form of pocket money, but it can be handed over in other ways too – as a Christmas or birthday gift, for example. Some teens also top up the funds they receive by non-formal employment, like walking the neighbour's dog or babysitting. How much do they get? 'For Year 9s, the biggest category is between $10 and $30 a week,' Cincotta says. That mirrors the evidence given by the girls across Australia: some got nothing, many received $20 a week. The rationale for receiving money fluctuated widely. Some students receive their weekly allowance and are not required to do any chores. Others need to iron, cook one night of the week, and clean their bedroom as part of that pay, which is docked if they don't. Another smaller group received pocket money until they snagged a part-time job. The pocket money stopped then, despite them being paid only marginally more in their jobs. Perhaps not surprisingly, most students were unified in believing they should get more. 'I get hardly anything,' they'd say. And some, perhaps mirroring the stance they've heard from their parents, don't expect pocket money. 'You do the jobs because you are part of the family, like making your bed. Why would you get paid for it?'

According to Commonwealth Bank research, almost 80 per cent of parents pay pocket money, with the average rate varying. Veronica Howarth, the head of school banking and youth at the Commonwealth Bank, says the average weekly pay packet for a teen aged between 13 and 15 years of age is $14.11. 'Our research also found that pocket money is given in exchange for work,' she says. The most common chores expected of teens are making their beds, keeping their rooms tidy, putting their belongings away, mowing the lawn, hanging out the washing and doing the dishes. In the Commonwealth Bank's research, about 13 per cent also received money as a reward for good marks at school.

So how might you decide to give pocket money to a 14-year-old? The ways are many, and there's no right or wrong if you ask company chiefs, educators and parents. Some connect it to chores, and some don't. Some increase it with each birthday, and others don't. But Arun Abey, chair of ipac securities limited and co-author of *How Much is Enough?*, suggests going about it this way: start by encouraging your teen to understand their role in a whole-of-house budget. The age of 14 is a good time to begin that, he says. He suggests sitting them down and genuinely outlining the costs of the entire household. That would include, for starters, electricity, rates, mortgage, food and water costs, private health fees as well as the costs associated with raising a child – school fees, clothing, sporting club fees and medical expenses, for example. The point of this exercise is that it allows transparency – so that your teen can see their part in the bigger scheme of things. The second step, according to Abey, is to agree on those elements of the budget that are non-discretionary. Of course parents would pay for school fees, electricity, food, rates, medical fees and family holidays, for example. The teen is then made to understand discretionary spending. This focuses their mind on how much money is put to entertainment, music downloads and concert tickets, for example. Encourage the teen to research what they believe is a fair discretionary amount of pocket money you should provide them. How many times would it be likely that they'd attend the movies in a month? What cost would they attribute to downloads? Should they go to a concert every couple of months? Often, Abey says, the child is blissfully unaware of those costs until this exercise is completed. On presentation of what the teen thinks is fair, a negotiation between parent and daughter should begin. Parents don't have to agree to everything – but this step allows the teen to understand the value of negotiation, too. It teaches teens that their parents can't afford to give them everything they want, and that money given to them is taken away from some other part of the household budget. Abey says parents also need to be committed to stick with the plan; it would not work if it was not enforced. 'I don't know about your boss, but if I overspend, by and large I can't go to my boss and say, "Sorry, I overspent. Will you increase my salary?"' Abey says.

That plan ticks many boxes. Apart from the obvious lessons, it shows the benefits of trading off, and mutes that curse many of us see in this generation of youngsters – immediate gratification. Cincotta, who was born in 1972, was brought up with her parents making her pay half of everything. 'I remember wanting to go to Queensland once and Mum and Dad [saying] if I saved up half the fare, [they] would pay for the other half.' The same went for a school excursion, at 15, to Japan. Her parents paid for the airfare, but she had to raise the spending money. One mother recently tried it, on a smaller scale, giving her 14-year-old daughter $70 a week but telling her that she was required to pay for a string of 'choices' she made, including milkshakes, ice-creams and hot chips or whatever else she decided to have with her friends after school, any 'unnecessary' clothing, a tennis lesson and friends' birthday gifts. 'Guess what?' she told me. 'All of a sudden the crap eating stopped.'

Arun Abey's approach does not carry any heavy reference to household chores, but you can see how your teen can learn a myriad of lessons. The first relates to understanding the running costs behind a home. It allows money to be visible, in a world where money is now largely invisible. Just on that point, think of your own childhood.

Some parents can remember, as a 14-year-old, their father coming home from work with cash in a pay packet. The money would then be put into a series of empty jam jars that were labelled: food, clothing, rent, holidays. And you could see it diminish over the fortnight. Some fortnights, nothing would go into the the holiday jar. Compare that to how your household budget might operate now, or how differently your own children learn about the value of money. From the youngest age, we take our children to the supermarket. The grocery trolley is filled. Plastic exchanges hands at the check-out, not money. Then, often, the operator will ask whether we also want cash out, and money is passed back to us by the cashier. In many ways, to young eyes, it looks as though we are being paid to go shopping. Cincotta agrees. 'We are living in a cashless society these days. The kids today talk about when Mum and Dad used to sign for things. Then Mum and Dad used to use a pin number, and now what Mum and Dad are doing is just tapping,' she says. More than half of students in any of her workshops raised their hands when asked whether their parents use tap cards. 'We are living in a cashless society and it's so easy to spend money, and they are growing up in that, so they just don't appreciate the value of money,' she says. (Many schools now also have cashless tuckshops). Veronica Howarth says the Commonwealth Bank's research had found that more than one third of younger children (35 per cent) didn't know the process behind paying for digital purchases. 'A lot of our research shows that children generally think that money comes from a hole in the wall,' she says. Indeed, 40 per cent of five-year-olds think you can use a card to get free money from an ATM, and 33 per cent of the same age group believe there's someone behind the wall who gives their parents the money. If only! The challenge, according to Howarth, is for parents to show that money has a real value.

Abey, who is also a director of the Smith Family, has a game worth playing with every teenager. It goes along these lines. Take a diary and give your 14-year-old (or any other age for that matter) a certain amount of money. The amount isn't really crucial to the game, because like real life, those from wealthy families will probably fork out more money to their teenagers than those from families who battle to make ends meet. The important thing, in this exercise, is that it's not a silly amount of money. So, for the purposes of this game, let's say it is between $30 and $50. The money should then be divided into two lots. The first lot should be used to buy a material good. But before your teen rushes off to pick up what they want, they need to use the diary to rate – out of 10 – how happy they believe that purchase will make them. Then let them buy it. Immediately after the purchase, they need to rate again – out of 10 – how happy their new purchase has made them. And then finally, a week later, they should retrieve the diary, and finish it off by logging how happy they are with their initial purchase. With the second lot of money, the teen needs to think of an experience. It might be a milkshake with friends after school, or a visit to the cinemas. It might be going to the local pinball parlour, or going camping – with the money used to pay for the experience. Before heading off to the 'experience', it's important to follow the same instructions outlined above. The teen writes down how happy the 'experience' will make them, on payment. They then record, on arriving home, how happy they are, before nominating a final rating, out of 10, a week later. The third and final element of the game doesn't have to involve any money (this is why you break the initial tally into two lots, not three). The teen needs to think of making, in Abey's words, 'a positive difference to somebody else'. 'It's what we call a letter of appreciation,' he says. 'Think of someone for whom you feel a genuine sense of appreciation; they've made a difference in your life. It could be a parent. It could be a friend. It could be a grandparent or a teacher. The important element is that it is genuine. Then your 14-year-old should sit down and write a letter of appreciation. It doesn't have to be long; three or four paragraphs should be enough to express why you feel that sense of gratitude. Once that's done, the teen needs to read the letter out loud to the target of their appreciation, in person. That means visiting the teacher or their rowing coach or their friend or grandfather. Like the two previous parts of the exercise, they then need to record how happy they think it will make them, out of 10. Immediately after visiting the person, and reading the letter, they make their second recording. And then, a week later, they make their final diary recording.

This is not an original game, as Abey points out. It's been played by university students the world over, as well as in many Australian schools. But almost always, irrespective of the teen's personality or socio-economic status or friendship groups, the results are the same. 'What you find, almost universally, is that before they buy the material thing – it could be a new CD or whatever – they'll say the material thing will rank 8 or 9 or 10 out of 10 in terms of expectations. Immediately after, it's pretty much still up there as well,' Abey says. 'But then, within a week, they'll discover a very strong decay factor.' A week later, the rating has plummeted. In terms of the experience, there's virtually no decay factor – so long as the teen purchased an outing or adventure they would genuinely like. 'The short lesson,' Abey says, 'is that things have a short shelf-life; experiences endure.' But the value of this experiment lies more in the letter of appreciation, read out to someone the teen feels really deserves it. The teen invariably believes that the letter-writing exercise will benefit the beneficiary more than them. Across the board, Abey says, it tended to rate low: about 5 out of 10.

'The other person's happiness would have been 10 out of 10.' Abey tells the story of a Sydney boy who wrote a note to his schoolmate. When he read it out, he was understandably nervous. Embarrassed even. But he did it. The schoolmate was silenced by the gesture, finally getting up and giving his friend a huge hug. But the important thing – and the moral of this – is that a week later, the teen author of the letter recorded in his diary 10 out of 10 for how it benefited him – double his initial expectation.

The power of generosity is well known, but it's not necessarily naturally understood. It's a learned skill. Or as Abey puts it, 'Our brains are wired for short-term surviving, not necessarily longer-term thriving.' That means our teens need to learn those cognitive skills like budgeting and saving on the one hand, but they also need to be guided into exercises that encourage the rewiring of their brains to understand emotional financial literacy – the relationship between money and wellbeing.

Cincotta believes as little as $10 or $15 is enough to begin a saving strategy. On her research, about three-quarters of students say they are saving money each week. But what does that mean? 'They say that they save it, but when I ask them how they save it, what they think about saving is that if they are not spending it, they're saving it. They think putting it in a money jar or a piggy bank – and there are some very cute responses, like hiding it under their bed – they consider that to be saving,' Cincotta says. She says there's no allocation or plan to the saving – except not to spend it, and about 56 per cent of students admit to having difficulty doing that. However, despite their ad hoc approach to saving, the target of any money they have is clear. Cincotta says clothing, accessories and shoes top the list each time, followed by travel, technology, concerts and gifts. She says the younger cohort – the 14-year-olds – show the most generosity in saving to give a present to someone else.

Here's a simple and effective savings strategy offered by Cincotta: open two bank accounts, with online access, so that the teen can log on and watch their wealth grow. No cards need to be attached to the accounts – especially one account – which means lower fees and higher interest. The aim is to have a direct debit facility between the accounts whereby money – as little as $5 a week – is moved from one to the other. (If that direct debit is set up automatically, it takes the discipline out of saving.) One account is the teen's normal savings account, where the money is lodged. The other is for the long-term saving – so part of their savings account is transferred regularly into that account. At schools, Cincotta introduced them to online calculators, something many of them show a fear of because they think it mirrors Maths. But what it does do is illustrate, in order to reach their goals, how much they need to put away each week – and that should be the amount for which they set up the direct debit. Once the required amount is saved (for that new skirt or concert tickets), it is transferred back to the normal account and spent. And the process starts again.

Remember how you were encouraged to save when you were young? In my case it was each Thursday, and with as little as $2 I'd march into the Commonwealth Bank to deposit it into my bank account. I'd proudly hand over the little dark blue book I kept by my bed, relishing the weekly stamps until there were so many it looked messy. Those stamps recorded how my money was growing. A generation on, Cincotta says students struggle with understanding the banking system, or how it makes money. 'For example, when I talk about the difference between cash and a term deposit – just having your money in your normal savings account versus giving it to the bank for six months – they'll say to me, "But why would the bank pay us more?"'

There's a reason – bigger than the next concert – for teen girls to understand finance. Look at any study and it points to them having lower superannuation levels, life-time savings below their male peers and, with one in two likely to divorce, a risk of greater debt along the journey. With four in five of this generation also expected to take a break from paid work to raise children, it's important to understand their place in context. But a crystal ball isn't needed to see that; the journey begins as children. A survey done for the Heritage Bank and released last year for International Women's Day showed school boys earned $13 a week – 35 per cent more than girls.[1] This is despite another survey – done by the Australian Institute of Family Studies – showing that girls, aged 10 and 11 in this case, did more housework than boys.[2] Cincotta says that at 14 it's probably too much to ask that students fully understand superannuation – but the link between the income they receive, their employment, and what they will end up with when they retire, is important. The research shows that at this stage teens still get their financial advice and guidance from their parents. 'There's research out there that says by the age of seven they've picked up their money habits from their parents and their relationship to money from their parents. I say to them that research shows that if Mum and Dad are on the right track financially, you will be as well. But the opposite is also true.'

That doesn't mean this generation won't face new challenges that their parents didn't. Saul Eslake says that many economists believe that the next generation might be the first one for more than a century who don't expect to live better than their parents. 'Most parents have expected and tried to ensure their children have better lives than they had. I think that was particularly a powerful aspiration for the depression generation, but it's by and large continued since then. That may now be changing,' Eslake says. He paints a different picture to the environment where these teens' parents thrived as teenagers. Our teens will experience a slower productivity growth, leading to slower economic growth. They'll also feel the weight of generations of debt. 'Some of the economic growth that most countries have experienced over the past 25 to 40 years has been funded by debt. It would seem that most societies have reached the upper limit of how much debt they can sustain relative to their income.' Our 14-year-olds won't work for the same employer or in the same occupation all their lives and need to be conscious that they do not need to acquire skills for a particular occupation but rather need the skills *and* the attitudes that will allow them to move from occupation to occupation. And their best chance of home ownership will come with an inheritance from their parents.

That last point is certainly highlighted in the Household, Income and Labour Dynamics in Australia survey which has used data from more than 17 000 Australians over 15 years. It found that fewer than half of all Australian adults are expected to own a home in the next few years.[3] 'Even in the 2011 census, home ownership was the lowest since 1954, and although it wasn't much below 1961, what's more striking than the decline in the overall home ownership rate is the very sharp decline in home ownership in people aged 25 and 55,' Eslake says. That means they will stay at home longer, or rent when they move out. It will be harder to start their own businesses because they won't have a house to put on the line to get the finance. 'It will ultimately also have an impact on retirement incomes because our retirement system assumes implicitly that the majority of retired people have close to zero housing costs.'

These facts can make for a gloomy picture. Indeed, the fact that home ownership might escape our teens will have an enormous impact on their lives. Home ownership for these teens' parents formed part of their culture; a form of self-expression that helped build their identities and connections to the communities they lived in. Our 14-year-olds might not have that luxury.

Education offers an upside to this view, however. Today's 14-year-old girls have only ever known a world where there are more university students that are female than male. Indeed, social researcher Mark McCrindle says the best measure of this is in the 25- to 34-year-old group, because they will have completed their university courses. 'If you look at 25- to 34-year-olds in Australia, 29 per cent of males in that age group have a university degree. Forty per cent of females in that age group have a uni degree,' he says. Generation Z would continue to smash those educational glass ceilings, being more likely to complete Year 12 as well as university. Normally, McCrindle says, income follows education. 'So this generation very likely will be out-earning the men in many fields, and that's the expectation of Gen Z girls – they've never known anything other than that. But it can also create a sense of dislocation of role and place,' he says. What can I, as a 14-year-old girl, offer? Is there a unique life stage for us? A particular offering we can make to society in the way our mothers might have? 'Access and empowerment are fantastic when they work,' McCrindle says, 'but have to be balanced with that sense of dislocation that could follow.'

Many 14-year-old girls get an early sense of what dislocation, or isolation, can feel like. To those individuals – and there are so, so many – it's meted out at lunchtime as the Mean Girls parade their power, lifting some and banishing others. They will do almost anything to feel as though they belong. *Almost* anything.

5

Beating loneliness

'I only have one friend left. No-one likes me,
even though I'm nice. I'm just not outgoing
enough. Too shy. Sometimes I look like an
idiot. My skin is having a breakout.'

TAYLOR,
14

Karen wanted $20 before she left for school, and her mother needed to know why. 'We're buying someone a present for their birthday,' her daughter offered. The fact that she said 'someone' and didn't refer to her friend by name sparked her mother's interest. Who was it? She saw an opportunity to engage her daughter, who now spent a touch too much time with her door closed, listening to music. 'Who's the lucky girl?' she asked. It was a girl Karen's mother had not met but was in the same year level at school. The pair shared the same circle of friends. 'What are you buying her?' Karen's mother asked. The answer: a $230 bottle of French perfume. 'I said, "I beg your pardon?"' The tone of the conversation changed abruptly. Everyone was putting in $20, her daughter said, becoming panicked. Her mother held her ground. She knew the birthday girl had never been to their home, and that Karen had not been invited to her party. 'Do you even hang around this girl?' Karen said she did; they weren't close but Karen was on the periphery of this friendship group, and really wanted to be part of it. 'I can't not do it, Mum. I've been asked to do it. They're counting on me.'

Karen's mother retells the story, still shaking her head. 'If I had a bottle of Chanel perfume at 14 I'd still have it, because I would have only used a drop at a time.' Her friend chimes in: 'I wouldn't have opened it. I would have just kept looking at it.' But, for now, forget the wisdom or otherwise involved in giving a 14-year-old a bottle of French perfume. Forget the comparison with when you might have been 14, and the chances your school friends would meet you at the bag rack with a bottle of French perfume. Even forget, again for now, what all the experts say about delayed gratification, and the need to work to enjoy $230 treats. 'The need for acceptance at this age is overwhelming,' Karen's mother says. 'These girls just have to fit in, at any cost.' If Karen didn't arrive at school with her $20, she risked being left out in the cold by her friends. And the way she described it, that was a fate akin to death.

The girls don't hide that. 'Fitting in' trumps almost anything else, including going to a party or having money to splurge. 'If you don't fit in, you are treated differently. If you don't fit in, basically you are a no-one,' another 14-year-old says.

That angst behind the girls' search for their tribe is raw and heartbreaking, and seems to reach a crescendo in the heart of high school. To 'belong', teachers say over and over again, they will change what they think and how they dress. 'The friends in our group change us as people,' explains one girl. 'For instance, if everyone in the group is doing choir, you feel pressure to do it as well.' Principals nod when you put that to them. To belong, girls will readily alter how they act and even how they speak. 'But, what is it about Year 9 that is important for them? What is the main issue for a girl at this age?' Those rhetorical questions are the start of a speech to Year 9 parents, delivered by Marise McConaghy, who is now principal of Strathcona Girls' Grammar School in Melbourne's inner eastern suburbs. She's referred to the subject of Year 9 girls a few times, as she's weaved her way up the education hierarchy. 'I am sure it is not news to any of you that the all-consuming concern of girls of this age is which group they are in or should or could be in, who they sit with at lunch, who sits next to them in class and whether or not someone or other kept them a place in class, and whether one girl or another spoke to them in some way or another that was deemed good, bad or yet to be defined . . .' Parents nod. Just as their daughters are bound by the need to 'fit in', they are bound by the need to deal with it, when things fall apart – not that their daughters see it that way. 'Fitting in wasn't a big deal when my mother was my age so she'd never understand that,' Kerrianne says. In one group of 16 girls, all attending a top-tier private girls' school, 14 of them nominated 'fitting in' as the single issue that determined their daily wellbeing.

Remember when your children were young, racing through the house at breakneck speed. Like you, I'd be constantly warning them to 'walk, don't run'. In the tween years they started walking – but that occasional skip still featured. But wait, some of my friends warned me, by 14 they start to drag their feet. McConaghy paints a similar picture at school. Cognitively, physically and emotionally our 14-year-old girls are changing, and that free-limbed excitement of childhood has been smothered by the need to grow up. 'I see the Year Sixers flying across the campus. They're still running and jumping and hopping,' she says. Like any parent, she'd like to bottle that, for just a bit longer.

'It's tough for parents too,' she says. She's speaking here as a parent-principal. 'In Year 9 they're not sure which group they're in and who likes them. They still want a best friend. There's a perfect friend out there for them and then they get let down because people are people and their supposed best friend finds another supposed best friend.' She says the power of groups, or tribes, has become greater over the past decade. 'It is interesting to speculate on why,' she tells parents. 'Could I suggest to you that even though we know that the girls need to separate from us and be with their friends, totally abandoning them to drown in the mire of 14-year-old minds is plainly foolish and actually negligent. They need to have boundaries around how much time they are with each other – either physically or in the cyber world – and they need to experience the boredom of the company of their parents and other grown-ups . . .'

Senior Constable Kelly Humphries sees the desperate attempts by teen girls to fit in every day. 'They have to be part of a group or part of something,' she says, 'and if they're not, they are isolated. They are left out. And they become completely disengaged.' Knowing this clientele better than most, she is nevertheless surprised at the bystander behaviour it prompts. 'I've never seen anything like it in my life. It's like if there's a fight on the oval, for instance. There's this pack of mice that run when the water is coming.' They arrive as a pack, all filming it. 'It's overwhelming,' she says. 'It's that herd behaviour.' No-one wants to stand out or be the person who is different from everyone else. The girls agree, even admitting to playing down their intelligence in some classes, joining in gossip they don't agree with – and, when prompted by Humphries' experience, even walking past someone being bullied in a bid to 'fit in'. The fact that they have these insights makes it harder to fathom.

'My middle one says she won't stand up to bullying in a crowd,' a mother tells me. 'She wouldn't walk in and stop it – unless it was an older person with a younger person.' Why? This mother has asked her 14-year-old that question over and over, and the answer remains the same. Her daughter says she wouldn't have the confidence or the strength, in front of a pack, to be the one to do something different. 'They think it would be turned on them and they don't want attention drawn to them,' she says. Teachers and school nurses see it daily: a group of girls, sitting around at lunchtime, wondering how to fill in their time. If they're not playing sport and they're not at debating practice, they need to do something. They're not interested in the monkey bars anymore, and the spectre of university and the need to fill their lunchtimes with catch-up classes or study seems a future away. 'And these groups of girls decide they will target someone,' one school nurse says. Faith, who goes to a country high school, admits she's often part of the problem. She hates herself, she tells me, but if everyone else turns on someone – even a girl passing their table to go to the tuckshop – it's easier to participate in the maligning than speak up against it. Why? 'They're my group,' she says. Tabatha, from a private school, says the same. 'I have found where I fit in and have created a view of the world for myself,' she says. But she lives on edge, fearful that any day could be the day that the group decides she is no longer part of it; that she'll be tossed out because she's not popular enough or pretty enough or funny enough. 'I'm clouded with the doubt that things can change really quickly and that people and things I love may change and I may not be happy in my future.'

Gossip is worth a mention here. Often, girls' friendships are driven by it. Even if it does start with a hint of accuracy, it quickly becomes a playground game of Chinese whispers. Girls admit they find it almost impossible to resist gossip, and make others feel on the outer if they don't join in. On a daily basis, around the lockers and over the lunch table, gossip takes on a life of its own, feeding an urge to fit in, often at any cost, and it's only the maligned and the very mature who don't become active participants. Another mother of a 14-year-old, who does teenage counselling as a day job, says the girls' group is part of their identity. 'It is who they are at school. It's absolutely huge,' she says. She knows that as a mother as much as a teen counsellor. 'The other day we were having a chat in the car when we pulled up at home and she said, "I don't know what's going on with my grade at the moment, Mum. Everyone seems on edge and they are all picking on each other and I don't know why,"' she relates. She could feel the dread rising in her daughter's voice as she articulated the problem out loud: her friends were picking on each other, groups were changing. When the music stopped, her daughter didn't want to be the one without a chair.

Speaking to girls across Australia, in public and private schools, the irony is explosive. They will fight for their opinion to be heard. Their grandparents' failure to understand climate change risked sending us all back to the Dark Ages. Why shouldn't the Constitution reflect the first Australians? Same-sex marriage was no longer a negotiation; that debate belonged to the last century. They are independent, stand their ground, demand to be heard. But turn the spotlight back on them and their views on their own world become as homogenous as their progressive arguments. They love the same clothes ('OMG, what about that new top Sarah wore to the movies; I've just got to have one!'), the same music, and they watch the same television shows. They'll work harder at school if their friends are working harder . . . and put in less effort if their friends are doing the same. They'll change the way they talk and take an extra risk or two 'if everyone else is doing the same'. They'll change who they are, for the sake of fitting in. Of course, that all-or-nothing thinking will pass as they climb through adolescence, and is partly due to the undeveloped brain described in Chapter 1. But while it lasts it can have massive reverberations on both their confidence and decision-making capabilities.

Perhaps, though, that urge to 'fit in' shouldn't surprise us, despite the heartbreak it spreads, given the training they have had up until this point. At a school fête a few years ago, young girls from the local ballet school were entertaining the masses. It was a jazz dance and they were all dressed in shimmery clothes, the glitter leaving fairy dust between the high kicks and leg splits that filled their 15-minute performance. The age of these children was difficult to pick but it turned out they were eight- and nine-year-olds. The mother next to me was perplexed. She had two sons, rowdy boys who were off lining up for the rides that turned your stomach upside down. You could see her frown, as she scanned the neat lines of dancers. 'How come they all have exactly the same hairstyle? Do they need to have hair like that to make it into competition?' She wasn't making a joke. With their hair universally pulled back hard in a single high ponytail, it was difficult to spot a single difference in hair length or hair style. Or make-up. Or costume. The shoes matched. The kicks were timed precisely; no-one was a step out in this choreographed performance. She repeated her question. 'I just don't understand it; do you have to have long hair to go to that dance school?' Those of us with girls laughed. Every dance mother knows the drill here.

'They're wearing hair pieces,' someone nearby explained, 'so they all look the same.' 'But why?' she asked.

If I could invite Andrew Fuller to my home every time I had a question about teenagers, I'd be a happy camper. A clinical psychologist, he authored *Tricky Teens* and his advice is constantly sought. So why, I ask him, do girls so desperately want to fit in? This age group, he explains, is enveloped by an 'all or nothing' type of thinking. 'If I fall out with my best friends then I'm never going to have a best friend again.' That's how this cohort thinks. Fuller is articulating both the fear and the thinking process.

Talking to Alex Curtis, from Kids Helpline, highlights that point. 'What we hear is, "That group isn't talking to me anymore so now I have to find another group."' The anxiety is serious enough, at least to these teens, for them to pick up the phone and want to talk to Kids Helpline. 'It comes back to that identity thing,' Curtis says. 'Where do I fit? Why don't I fit with that group?' Curtis could pull any case study from her files, but Piper, 14, from Victoria, illustrates her point. Piper first contacted Kids Helpline in December 2015. She was distressed, crying throughout the call. She told the counsellor how she had thought of jumping out of a moving car. She wanted help. Why? The isolation she felt at school. Surrounded by classmates, she felt alone. She'd been bullied previously – and that had included a group spreading rumours about her. She had become socially isolated. And she could not remember the last time she'd had fun.

Even for girls with warm and connected relationships at home – and that is many – biological drivers connect them most strongly to their own age group, says parenting guru Maggie Dent. That's at least the case with children who *do* have friends. If they don't, she says, 'they'll do anything to belong.' Dent says doing risky things or breaking rules can be motivated by a plea for acceptance. 'Girls will become sexually active, they'll take drugs, they'll do whatever they can to fit with someone their own age,' she says. 'That's a little bit frightening because if you're an academic girl or a social girl or whatever you are, you go, "Phew, I fit here," but if you're on the fringe and you don't fit in any of those places – they are the at-risk kids.' Police agree. Often, the girls couldn't see past the crisis, which amounted to being frozen out of a group of friends. 'And they haven't got that resilience to deal with the problem,' Senior Constable Kelly Humphries says. 'They haven't got those pathways or strategies because they haven't been taught them.'

The proof of that is in the figures. Andrew Fuller and Andrew Wicking, with Resilient Youth Australia, have surveyed 91 369 young Australians in Years 3 to 12. 'In Years 3 to 12, 43 per cent of students (47 per cent of girls and 40 per cent of boys) have good or high levels of resilience,' they say. However, there was a steady drop from 59 per cent of students reporting good or high levels in primary school to 27 per cent of students in Years 11 to 12.[1] Fuller and Wicking nominate 'belonging' as the most powerful antidote to suicide, violence and drug abuse. 'The sense of belonging at school is strong in the primary years, with girls having a stronger sense of belonging than boys,' they say. 'Over the secondary/high school years it drifts so much that by Years 11 to 12, 23 per cent of girls and 26 per cent of boys have a low sense of school belonging.' That is less than one-quarter of the school community!

Fuller and Wicking, in breaking it down to specific years, say Years 7 and 8 represent the time when, despite a great surge in cognitive ability, 'the engagement seen in Years 5 to 6 slows and lessens, positive connectedness weakens and achievement levels in numeracy and literacy languish.' There were girls who were very successful in Year 6, Fuller tells me, who 'tend to fall quite alarmingly by Year 7 and Year 8.' But worse is to come. Year 10 is when the lowest levels of resilience occur, according to their survey. 'It coincides with increased feelings of alienation and disconnection. While the origins of this low point may occur earlier through not establishing close positive relationships or having a sense of success at school, Year 10 is the pinch point.' Fuller says Years 9 and 10 are the time when learning should refocus on real life. Areas that can help are robotics, coding, commerce, forensics, analysis of local business, working on future projects, virtual technologies and drama. 'By Years 9 and 10 we have a group of students who feel disengaged from school and are relatively impervious to classroom-based interventions. This means that while building resilience curricula should still be implemented, it will only go so far.'

At Abbotsleigh, an Anglican pre K–12 school for girls in New South Wales, it has been Drama, year after year, that has proved effective in dealing with some of those Year 9 issues around the need to fit in. The 'bump year', as Head of Senior College Annette Ware calls it, was stuck between the excitement of starting high school and graduation, and the difference in the cohort varied too, from young girls still enjoying their childhood to sophisticated young women on the brink of adulthood. 'It can be a sort of treading-water year,' she says. So the school, more than a decade ago, started the Wheeldon Cup Project, an annual performing arts project that is entirely student driven. It involves every student in Year 9, divided into four teams of between 30 and 40 students each. The emphasis of the project, which is created, rehearsed and performed in public twice, is on the process. The only staff involvement is the selection of a theme. It might be *Women of Worth from History* or *Blessed are the Peacemakers*, for example. The students then need to allot roles: research team, director and assistant directors, treasurer, environmental monitor, choreographer, musical directors, stage managers, lighting, sound, IT designers, operators. Together they nut out a plan, create the costumes, write the music, choreograph the dances and practise. The budget is limited, with each student contributing just $2 – meaning there is a maximum of $80 for each group to spend.

The results, Annette Ware says, have been spectacular, and it has taught the students to value and respect the input of other students they might have previously walked past in the playground. Each role has to be performed well for the production to shine. Ware says that at 13 and 14 it is often the good-looking, sporty, extroverted girls that reign at the top of the social pyramid, but this project showcases the value and talents of everyone. 'There's a beautiful sense of girls not only identifying their own strengths but being able to identify and value the strengths of other people,' she says.

The same type of program – taking the Year 9 cohort away from the rest of high school and teaching them life skills – is now practised far and wide, albeit in different ways. Perhaps the most well known case is that of Geelong Grammar School's Timbertop program, where students camp out for between 50 and 55 nights during the year. In addition to their daily classes, students ski, canoe, raft, camp and hike in terrain that is mountainous, with routes sometimes involving ascents and descents of 1000 metres – all in one day.

Educators say it won't be long before schools the length and breadth of Australia – public and private – will attempt to treat Year 9 girls in a different way. Many in Queensland say the urgency of the task has increased since Year 7 was transferred into high school. At least two big schools in Queensland are already debating how it might happen – and are looking to the experience of schools in Victoria to develop a plan.

Here are two examples. For the past quarter of a century, Methodist Ladies' College in Victoria has sent its Year 9 students to a 114-hectare farm, bordered by the Croajingolong National Park and the Mallacoota Inlet, in far East Gippsland. There, at Marshmead, the College's remote residential campus, about 70 students each term live for eight weeks in a small village. Living together in groups of eight, the students prepare their own menus, within nutritional guidelines, order the food they need within a set budget, cook their meals, and clean their own accommodation. Lisa Gatliff, the director of student wellbeing, says some students might never have washed a dish because they'd always used a dishwasher. On this program they learn to step outside their comfort and knowledge zones to develop strong life skills. Daniel Short, the college's director of outdoor education, says that sometimes the students remark on how they never realised how much work their parents did behind the scenes. 'The laundry. The washing. The cooking.'

The driving principle, Short says, is for students to explore their own role in promoting a sustainable future, and that is looked at from a personal, environmental and community level. Discussions and investigations about the use of water and electricity, for example, replace formal science and maths classes. 'They arrive back in Melbourne with a new sense of maturity, a new sense of self-awareness and a new sense of independence, and I would say they also come back with a new sense of what their priorities are,' Short says. 'We remove so many distractions when we are at Marshmead.' Students are unable to access emails and social media platforms, and computer use is limited to checking weather sites, for example. Make-up is left in Melbourne, and the focus on what they look like takes a back seat to feeding a poddy calf, turning the compost, chopping wood and keeping the fires stoked. Phone calls are only allowed on birthdays, and the main form of communication for the period is hand-written letters. Lisa Gatliff says that without the distraction of mod-cons, students often take up knitting and play board games. At the end of the day, tired and without distractions, it's rare for a student not to sleep for a full eight hours. 'Some of the simple things that they have totally discarded they come back to and see the benefit of ... That's really wonderful,' she says.

Students return to school with a real sense of 'fitting in' – not just with their old friendship groups but with the broader class. 'If they've got a good friend who is going in a different term, then they can spend half the year apart from one another [because of the rotations],' Gatliff says. Friendships evolve. 'It really expands their friendship networks and they have this connection that lasts for the rest of their school experience and beyond.' Gatliff has also seen another upside, where, away from the normal groupings, different children can flourish. She gives the example of one student who spent time at Marshmead a few years ago. She was passionate about music but lacked the confidence to perform in public. Over the weeks, she started to perform in front of her peers at Marshmead. In Years 10 and 11 she relished public performances, and by Year 12 she was earning good money doing gigs around Melbourne. 'In Year 9 she couldn't see that she could possibly do that,' Gatliff says. 'That's a beautiful example.'

While many other examples exist, Strathcona Girls' Grammar School in Victoria – a private Baptist school catering for early learning through to Year 12 – takes a slightly different approach in dealing with the Year 9 cohort. The girls are based at a different campus for the entire year – a mansion by the Yarra River. As day students, they travel to and from their campus each day. They are encouraged to develop their independence by catching public transport. While the academic focus features interdisciplinary projects targeting Melbourne, the year is also used to develop new bonds, issue challenges to the students, increase their resilience and build independence.

Strathcona principal Marise McConaghy says role models play a significant part in helping girls find their individuality and their tribe. She says they often pretend they don't need their parents anymore, at that age, but it's just not true. 'I'd walk around the table and you'd pretend you weren't hearing what they were talking about, but they were talking about their parents. "My father thinks this" and "my mother thinks this",' she says. Role-modelling by more senior students was also vital, and she believed it was important to have several 'captains' in Year 12 to envelop all those wanting role models. 'The captain of sport might be loved by the confident, sporty girls, but another shy girl, who's not so great at sport, might not be inspired – might even be intimidated by her as a role model,' she says. McConaghy supports music and service and debating captains and says that school captains and their deputies, from her experience, rarely boasted similar attributes. 'That's really good, too; they can see, "Oh I couldn't be like that but I *could* imagine being like that,"' she says.

An outside-school example of challenging Year 9s to see the value of not always fitting in is offered by World Challenge, a personal development program offering student experiences in 40 different destinations, from Vietnam and Cambodia to Ecuador, Tanzania and Botswana, for example. South-East Asia is the strong favourite for Australian students. Mark Walters, general manager of World Challenge, says the demand, historically, came from students in Years 10 and 11. 'But more and more we're getting requests from schools to engage part of their Year 9 cohort, or in some cases their entire Year 9 cohort, to go away,' he says. Started 30 years ago, the two to three-week program provides accommodation for the students for the first night, then they have to nut out the details of their accommodation, budgets, transport and community engagement. The focus is fairly and squarely on the student's personal development.

All of these programs have, as their central tenet, a focus away from self and towards team; a drive to look outwards, not inwards. And not all of them find it easy. 'Some of the girls can't slice a tomato before they go,' says the principal of another such program. 'A lot of them try to get out of it because they don't want to sleep out or get out of their comfort zone. I think there's a lot to be said for giving them a focus, other than a preoccupation with each other's boyfriend's lives, and what they're wearing.'

While many of these programs have run for 30 years or more, the consequences of not 'fitting in' have never been greater. Perhaps that's because, in the past, the absence of social media meant the loneliness of being left out didn't follow us home. Or perhaps a greater emphasis sat on the ability to cope with boredom; to spend time by ourselves. But whatever the difference in generations, 14-year-olds today see it as an almighty chasm that their parents don't really understand. These students know they need to find the strength not to 'fit in' at any cost; to step up and stop a bullying incident; to wear their hair boy-short if they want to. But putting it into practice is so much more difficult.

Often it can come down to the group, or the tribe, where they fit. Take the example of the 14-year-old party held in a shopping centre. Tara's mother went to great lengths: it was a treasure hunt, with milkshakes along the way, offering equal doses of independence, teamwork and fun. Tara's friends, divided into pairs, had to find different markers, buy specific things, follow clues and return to a designated place within a required time. Tara's mother watched the girls take their clues and embark upon the activity. Her daughter's ballet friends, used to working together, decided upon their pairs and set off. They ran to the first clue, like young children. She could hear the squeals of delight. Tara's other friends, a group from school who didn't belong to any particular organised activity, got 10 metres down the shopping centre, stopped at the nearest coffee shop and sat there for the two hours, only returning when the game was due to finish. Tara's mother's theory is this: a team (dance, hockey, debating, whatever) enables girls to find a group who share a similar interest, allowing them to share in a spirit or focus where individualism is second to the teamwork. And that has to be a good thing.

In reality, however, that's not necessarily so. Paul Dillon from Drug and Alcohol Research Training Australia (DARTA) says sport and music could play a 'protective' role, but there was always a flip side. 'You only need a couple of influential people in a sport team to make a girls' team become a complete alcohol mess,' he says. Dillon's point is that sport and music could play a beneficial role in teen girls finding their 'tribe' but the wrong group could mean the exact opposite. A group of girls that gel together in a bad way could encourage drinking and other risky behaviour.

Ballet and athletics, where winning and losing can come down to a split second, require such intense focus that they can provide a protective role – more so than team sports where you can be not on your best game, and still win. This is slightly different to choir and music, which often attract students who are less likely to get into trouble in the first place, thus providing positive reinforcement to one another.

Andrew Fuller adds this rider. Many children don't like sport or don't want to be part of a team, so encouraging your child into a team, in the hope of finding them the right place to fit in, isn't necessarily a panacea. Fuller believes the answer lies in providing teens with the resilience they need to deal with situations. He says he's learnt, through research, that you can tell people about resilience but that's not the same as adding it to their toolbox. He says schools boast curricula where students are taught about resilience, but the worry there was that girls, largely compliant, will sit and nod their heads, and not learn. It was only when they were taught to act it out – by changing other people's lives – that they really understood it.

My father-in-law once told me that you share your children with their peers the moment they first walk through the school gates. His point was that a parent's authority dips as the pull of friendships takes over, and that pull grows stronger as your child grows up. He was right. Sometimes that is marvellous for a child. Other times it's not, and it can mean heartache and extreme isolation as pecking orders are built to shut some teens out.

6

The Mean Girls, The Nerds and The Rest

'A lot of people think we are all bitches but really we're not, and they think we're the "popular" group.'

SALLY,

14

Cady Heron is delightfully unpretentious and unsophisticated when she trots off to her first day at an all-American high school, as a 15-year-old, in the 2004 movie *Mean Girls*. Up until that point, she'd been home-schooled by her zoologist parents in Africa, learning her lessons amongst the wildlife. She's naive to the intimidating pecking order that exists in the school playground, and quickly turns and asks her new friends, 'Who are the plastics?' They were talking about a small group of attractive teen girls, strutting their short skirts, surrounded by a gaggle of admirers. Oh, they're school royalty, she's told, before being warned of their other attributes. Karen Smith was one of the 'dumbest' girls you will ever meet. 'She asked me how to spell "orange",' her friend says. Gretchen Wieners, the one with the big hair and the midriff, was 'totally rich' thanks to her daddy. 'She knows everyone's business. She knows everything about everyone,' she's told. 'That's why her hair is so big,' another chimes in. 'It's full of secrets.' And the third was the school's queen bee, Regina George. 'She may seem like your typical selfish, back-stabbing, slut-faced ho-bag, but in reality she's so much more than that.' Regina George is revered and feared in equal measure.

'Regina George is flawless,' one student in *Mean Girls* says. 'She has two Fendi purses and a silver Lexus,' says another. 'I hear her hair's insured for $10 000,' another again says.

'I hear she does car commercials – in Japan,' says yet another.

'One time she punched me in the face. It was awesome,' a final girl says.

It's a parody of high school, but strikingly similar to the characters and roles being played out in Australian high schools today. From day one, Cady finds the teen jungle much harder to navigate than any in Africa. The school strata structure hangs over the teens, determining who they speak to, how they dress and even what tables they lunch at: the jocks sit together; so do the preps, and the Asian Nerds, and the Cool Asians, and the Varsity jocks, the unfriendly black hotties, the girls who eat their feelings, the girls who don't eat anything, the desperate wannabes, the burnouts, the plastics. The list goes on. *Mean Girls* was loosely based on the 2002 self-help book *Queen Bees and Wannabes: Helping Your Daughter Survive Cliques, Gossip, Boyfriends and the New Realities of Girl World*, by Rosalind Wiseman. And it's easy to laugh along at some of the characters' lines. But tomorrow those lines could be delivered by any of our daughters. Some of them will be in the Plastics, or the Too Cool group, that reign like royalty. Others will hang to its fringes, pleading to be lifted onboard. Others will be ostracised, ignored – or worse, ridiculed. It's hard in real life, and Cady showed that on screen. 'Why didn't they [her parents] just keep home-schooling you?' she's asked. 'They wanted me to get socialised,' she responded. 'Oh, you'll get socialised all right,' comes the retort.

In Australian high schools, the groups rarely differ. This is how our 14-year-olds see it:

'The academic girls sit together. The TCs (Too Cools) sit together. And then there are the rest.' – TINA, 14

'The popular girls and the nerds and geeks.' – LIZZIE, 14

'*I am basically part of the rather larger geeky group but we take pride in it. We had a couple of other groups merge with us.*' – SAM, 14

'*There are the populars, nerds, friendly smart people, try-hards and the nasties.*' – RUBY, 14

'*There're the nerdy/brainy/smart people and the popular/ social media type of people.*' – JULIE, 14

'*Popular, nerdy, weird, boy-crazy and normal – the in-betweens.*' – ALISON, 14

'*There're the popular boys and the popular girls and they start to date each other. Then there are the geeks and they are really brainy. And then there's our group. We have lots of the leadership roles because we're in the middle. We're not in the popular group but we're not outcasts.*' – REBECCA, 14

'*Our group is mostly high-achieving and academic. I suppose we'd be classified as nerds. The rest of the grade is more 'with the trends' and they are classified more normal. Our group is sometimes looked at weirdly but there seems to be a sort of respect for us from the rest of the grade.*' – ELLIE, 14

'*Most of them know each other from primary school and they walk around like they are queen bees. They're not called populars because everyone likes them. At my school, last year, they would call themselves the Plastics or the Mean Girls. They thought that was a good thing. They called themselves the Plastics!'* - VONNIE, 14

The fact that they all largely agree on the group types is fascinating enough, but the girls' ability to roll out quick definitions of their year's groupings shows how entrenched they are, and how unremarkable the labels are, to the girls. Not one teen girl said groups didn't exist; and even their descriptions are devilishly close to each other. Sometimes teens fall, naturally, into a group and 'belong'. Other times they search for a crowd where they feel they can be themselves. Many of them try to attain the 'status' of a TC; some are welcomed into that group on a whim, and devastated when they are discarded just as quickly. (Despite most girls wanting to be a TC, they will not admit that and even feel slighted if accused of being one!) It's ruthless and can make or break a girl's day. Some girls sit on the outer of a group by choice. Others don't want to go to school because they just can't find where they belong. Indeed, school refusal didn't exist as a problem five years ago; now it is a serious and growing problem, according to Karen Spiller, the experienced education leader.

Another principal has had that personal experience with her 14-year-old niece. 'She's very bright, plays the violin, but has missed the last term of school,' she says. The whole term. 'We were talking about it and it came down to friends. There had been a falling out.' It was spectacular: she was no longer welcome in her group. That meant she was isolated. Going to school became unbearable. 'She couldn't face school,' this principal says. 'It became a real school refusal. That anxiety over relationships and friendship is so strong.' And what was the falling out over? 'Who supported Hillary Clinton and who supported Bernie Sanders.'

The irony of that is spectacular. These girls can be intelligent and opinionated enough to spend a lunchtime arguing about politics, but then struggle to deal with the fact of someone having a different view to their own. Some girls couldn't countenance a day in the schoolyard without the sense of belonging to a tribe. 'The girls in my circle mean the most to me and I'd be lost without them,' Sienna, 14, says. 'And there can be a lot of protocols involved when you want to leave one group and join another,' a principal says. 'I've heard of situations where girls have actually requested permission to leave the group. It is real. It is that very tribal thing.'

I sought the views of dozens and dozens of girls and every one was able to classify the Year 9 groups at her school. Every one. And they fell into similar groupings. The populars or the TCs (Too Cools). They were also called the Queen Bees, the Plastics, the Boy-Crazies. They had the best clothes, and were often viewed as the prettiest. Sometimes they did well in class and some didn't, but what drew them together was how they looked and what they could laud over the others. Their interest in boys was strong, as was their communication on social media. Many of these admitted to having boyfriends, and some were seeing them without their parents' knowledge.

The second clear group were the Nerds, also known as the Academics, or the Geeks, or the Smarts. The name varied but the attributes didn't. School work over social life. They wanted to do well. Their parents wanted them to do well. Their clothes, often, were a bit old-fashioned. Every Asian girl I talked to belonged to this group. These girls don't care much whether their 'look' fits with expectations. They might have short hair, where the others wore copycat ponytails. They race to coding club at lunch, and don't mind pulling out an old and unfashionable lunchbox from their school bag. The third big group was the most fluid. Sometimes it was full of 'the others' – girls who didn't easily slot into either of the other big groups. Sometimes this group is divided into the sporty types and the arts types. Often this is the group where a child can be most happy and most uneasy. It's also the group, many principals say, that throws up the school leaders.

That might be the three broad groupings, but it's a bit like going to the bakery to buy your favourite cheesecake and finding it not there. Do you take the chocolate torte? The cream-filled sponge? Or the fruit loaf? Sometimes girls don't know what they want, or where they'll fit. They might want to be a TC, but be more naturally aligned to the geek group. And in many of those cases, they'll just hang on the periphery, desperate to be 'chosen' to join in.

Orientation rituals (for the TC group) can include all sorts of behaviour, depending on the school, the state and the latest fad, but the girls in some cases report having to swear publicly and loudly, back-answer a teacher, trip a peer, take someone's lunch or slap another girl across the face. Sadly, many of them oblige; and few girls admit no longer wanting to join a group because of its 'entry' requirements. In other schools and states, none of this exists. The groupings get along, as you would hope, and are much more welcoming to those who feel they don't 'fit in' anywhere else.

Principals, teen psychologists and parenting experts say the group or tribal gatherings inside the school yard play a crucial role in the natural separation process between teenager and parents. It is a normal part of growing up, they say, that girls should seek to find their own identity. Membership of a group offers a way of doing that. Inside the safe embrace of their friends, they feel comfortable enough to 'try out' who they want to be, adopting some of the values and views of their parents, and dispensing with others.

One of the many inconceivable issues here is how strong, independent girls become slaves to compliance and silly talk, preferring being popular with boys over their peers. The girls know that. Indeed, they raise it, and it no doubt rankles them as much as it does their parents and teachers. But the pull to belong, to have a tribe of friends who have your back, wins out almost every time. An upset can mean marks plummet. 'The neuroscience for girls is very, very clear on this,' Karen Spiller says. 'If a girl is not emotionally calm and stable she cannot learn. If she's had an argument with a buddy or feels a loss for whatever reason, and something that happens at lunchtime, we have to put all of our efforts into calming her down and sorting it out because she cannot study in the afternoon. It is physically not possible.' The girls agree. Ask them to rank their worries and 'friendships or relationships at school' exceeds bullying, schoolwork, body image and diet.

> *'At the start of this year a girl who was my only friend in class left our group and stopped talking to me. I started feeling very left out and down about myself. I didn't tell anyone for a few terms. One of my teachers finally noticed and I ended up exploding in a ball of tears.'* - MADDISON, 14

> *'I didn't realise it but friendship problems are very big around the age of 14. You seem to fight a lot more with your friends than earlier.'* - MIA, 14

'We changed our friendship group this year. We got sick of the drama. Everyone was about social media. They defined themselves by social media. It was like, "OMG my boyfriend hates me!" It was all a big drama. Or they find a celebrity on social media and go, "OMG I love him. I heart him. I'm going to marry him." The three of us just drifted into a new group.' – GEORGINA, 14

'Sometimes it's really bad, like when there was legal action [a restraining order] and parents were fighting with each other.' – KRISTIE, 14

'I had a best friend who was in all of my classes last year and we were very close – but not this year. She's really athletic and sporty and I'm into the arts, and then I started to hang out with my friends from dance troupe and stuff and then she starts to have friends from netball. It can be [hard] because we were so close, but I have made some lovely friends and we have similar interests.' – CHLOE, 14

That last comment, from a student in Tasmania, points to a picture that Jody Forbes, school psychologist and student counselling coordinator at Brisbane Girls' Grammar School, uses to describe the changing groups. 'I often use the lava lamp as an analogy to educate girls about relationships,' she says. Forbes says it can be on day three of the first year of high school that the girls feel as though they've missed the friendship bus. 'The girls will say all the groups have already been set,' she says. 'I've missed my shot. Everyone's already in a group and I can't get in.' Relationships aren't fixed; they ebb and flow constantly. 'Very few people form a group on the first day of school and spend the next five years being best friends with the same group of girls.' Forbes's lava lamp analogy is perfect. 'A bit comes and it separates then that bit goes and it splits into three and then that bit comes together. I say, you will always be forming and connecting, and the groups are fluid.' She wants the girls to know there will be constant opportunities to join one group or leave another. 'I talk to the girls about being friendly, even if they are not friends, because if you kick that girl out of this group – if you write a list and say, you're in and you're out – that might be the very girl, in six or 18 months' time, who is in the group that you need to join because you've been kicked out of [your] group.' There's another point here that Forbes – and several principals – mention. The head girls or the school captains are rarely the class's most popular girls, or the smartest. A student vote means it usually goes to girls who have proved to be friendly, time and time again, over the duration of high school. 'If that girl was nasty to you four years ago, you won't vote for her,' one principal says. These teens remember that sort of stuff.

This is a far cry from how things might have played out when their parents, particularly their mothers, went to school. I asked most of the principals I interviewed about their own high school days. They remember playground spats. Arguments that lasted a couple of days. But none of them remember really finite groups that girls had to enter and leave, a bit like entering and leaving a room. The factor at play here is that friendship groups, circa 2017, are relentless; there's no escaping them. When most of us were growing up, home was a sanctuary. It was 'down-time'. It closed the door on any school-yard arguments. That's not possible now. It does not stop. Before-school activities mean the girls are mixing, sometimes, at 5 am. After-school activities – from netball to hockey to theatre practice – means they are living in each other's pockets until after the sun goes down. And when they get home, finally, their phone remains on. And that means any altercation continues, and often escalates, overnight.

How schools deal with this varies as much as the orientation rules in joining a particular group. Jody Forbes says that the relational bullying between girls is often the result of their failure to deal with anger. 'Girls have no idea what to do with their anger – they are told from a young age to "play nice".' That often means it is very hard for them to be assertive and tell someone they feel upset by that person's actions. 'We must teach girls to be assertive, not just with peers when they are 14, but with future relationships – partners and colleagues, etcetera.' Dr Maree Herrett, principal of Santa Sabina College in Sydney's Strathfield, says a friendship room operates at her middle school, where students can come in and talk problems out with a mediator. The students sit on a cushion and really listen to the other person. They don't have to leave the room best friends, but a requirement exists to treat each other respectfully. Like many schools, Santa Sabina also has rollcall or home rooms. That usually means the student's home room caters for Years 7 to 12, and mixing up the ages tends to reduce friendship issues. However, as one parent quipped, there's a downside to that. 'I didn't really expect my 12-year-old to come home saying she was going to need $750 in a few years to buy her semi-formal dress!'

Other educators suggest steering your child towards another specific activity, in a bid to reduce friendship frictions. Says one principal, 'If they do music they're not always with their same age group. TCs tend to all be the same age. Sport offers a sanctuary for many, because it can involve girls from other schools as well.' Julie Warwick, principal of Robina State High School – a big public co-educational school on Queensland's Gold Coast – agrees. When asked what the biggest challenge facing 14-year-old girls is, her response is quick: 'Other 14-year-old girls. Sometimes they can be their own worst enemies.' She says engagement and keeping the students busy helps put a lid on the fallout from groups. She says her focus is on doing everything she can to foster really strong relationships between teachers and students, to foster a high-expectations environment where girls can work hard, to support positive behaviour and to support strong attendance. Add-on programs, like community-service responsibilities, were truly worthwhile but needed that sense of 'belonging' to the school to work. 'Peers are everything. Absolutely everything at this age. The starting point has got to be creating an environment in the school where a 14-year-old wants to be there, that they feel a sense of belonging and achievement, and that they set personal goals,' she says.

At Fahan School in Hobart, Tasmania, community work is used as a focus – whether it's a women's shelter, a local Variety club, visiting the sick or helping out the homeless. Social justice groups can be popular with this passionate lot, partly because they provide context and encourages the Year 9 cohort to look beyond the next social media crisis. Tony Freeman, principal at the school, is a big fan of this type of focus. 'It develops a sense of belonging,' he says. 'It helps their self-identity, and their independence. And they learn how easy it is to do something really constructive for others.' Teen psychologist Andrew Fuller believes that, for girls, the difference lies in them *doing* something rather than learning something. He says many teachers stand in front of a class and teach girls by talking to them. The girls don't have to be involved and can act compliant. It was only through practical work – 'doing' rather than just 'listening' – that the girls could see the power to change others' lives. 'It's through action that they learn their identity,' Fuller says.

The lessons learned through being ostracised can help build resilience. Freeman says many girls will try to become members of the cool group but soon come to the realisation that they won't be accepted, and that process helps them 're-establish their identity'. In the long run, the friendship groupings reduce in importance.'I quite often get parents coming in and saying, my daughter is having trouble, she's bitching with this person, and this person is being nasty. I just say wait till Grade 10,' Freeman says. 'A lot of times, the queen bees in Grade 8 aren't the queen bees in Grade 10, or those you assume to be the queen bees in Grade 8 are quite nice people and they settle in to who they are.'

Karen Spiller and her school leadership team ran 'carpet conversations' with different years, asking them about the issues they're facing. She usually oversaw the Year 12 conversation. 'What you get every single year is a comment about "We've rubbed up against each other in Years 9 and 10, we were very cliquey back then, but now we kind of understand,"' she says. They continue to have a best friend or a close circle of friends, but the rancour disappears. They understand each other. Other principals agree. When she was principal at Somerville House in Brisbane, Flo Kearney says her Year 12 cohort had an annual laugh at the final assembly over the angst of Year 9. 'Everybody gets it,' she says – even the Year 9s as they sit in class for the first time. 'The students going into Year 9 are aware that it is a tricky year. There's probably only a subset of Year 9 that we really do need to help through these friendship issues . . .'

A complexity can arise, however, when parents join in the group fights – which is surprisingly frequently. In some cases, parents have taken on other parents in the school car park, or even taken out legal action to ensure a child stays away from their own. 'You can't pick your child's friends,' principal Julie Warwick says. 'We've all tried to do that.' Another principal says parents often fuel the problems. 'We have parents who have [a kind of] Munchausen syndrome by proxy,' the principal of one elite girls' school told me. 'I think they want there to be a crisis with their daughter.' Another principal says, 'Parents are my worst clientele.' Often parents will seek external consultants to argue their point. In one case a mother had sought the advice of three different psychologists in a bid to get one of them to support her view.

Of course it can be hard for parents, too. Jim Rohn, American entrepreneur and author, coined the phrase that 'you are the average of the five people you spend the most time with'. In Year 9, who is that for your child? What often makes it worse is that parents have a stake in this. School fees are huge, and often the motivation to send a child to a good school is driven by a parent's desire to develop a calibre or network of solid, good friends.

Sometimes a group can turn on one of its own, just so that others in the group can feel more secure. However it plays out, there is no doubt it often envelops the girl's parents as well. They imagine her sitting by herself in class or wandering the school at lunchtime looking for a friend. But the advice from experts here is unanimous: how you react can make the situation worse. Stay calm and refuse to become angry or anxious over episodes of loneliness that your daughter might confront. In the words of one principal: 'You must not let her despair drown out your good sense.'

Sometimes, the girls say, admitting they talk to their parents about school-yard arguments can make matters worse at school. 'Most of my friends don't have the same relationship that me and my mum have,' says one girl. 'We're really close, but some of them are more secretive, and when I say I was speaking to my mum about this, they say, "Why are you speaking to your mum about that?" or "Don't tell your mum that I said this." That comment surfaced several times; sometimes girls are shunned because they might 'pass information on' to their parents.

It's a phase and unfortunately it adds to the media picture of our 14-year-old girls being bitchy. That rankles Joby Forbes. 'It's concentrated [amongst this age group], but your whole life, whether it's your mother-in-law, your sister or your boss, you're going to have to work out how to get along with people. That's why when parents say, "My girl's been bullied, you've got to stop that," we need them to learn how to navigate relationships themselves because it's not just now. It might be in Year 9 when they're 14, but it's also when they're 24 and 34.'

7

Mum and Dad know best. Not!

*'I don't want to bother them with my problems
when they have their own. I keep to myself.'*

KARA,

14

Two 40-something mothers are sitting in a cafe, their English Breakfast teas going cold but neither of them noticing. They chat like old friends, but have only ever fleetingly acknowledged each other in the school car park before today. But, on this afternoon, as the barista banters with the regulars, these two women are drawn to each other like age-old buddies. They swap stories, finishing each other's sentences, and find solace in someone else sharing their bumpy adventure.

Mother 1: 'I just have to look at her and she starts to cry. I'm exhausted.'

Mother 2: 'At least yours is crying. Mine just bites my head off. She says, "Why are you annoying me? Why are you hassling me? Why can't I do this?" When did it change from "Can I do this?" to "I am doing this, anyway"?'

There's a knowing nod.

Mother 1: 'It's like her whole focus has left the family and turned to her friends.'

Mother 2: 'I get a lot of the eye rolling. It's like, "this is boring" or "you are so uncool". We must have done that to our parents too, don't you think?'

Mother 1: 'I don't think they're any worse than I was at that age, but they're more disconnected now. Or disengaged from the family. Besides, there was only one phone in our house, so a mother could eavesdrop and know what was going on.'

Mother 2: 'I didn't talk back to my parents. I might have questioned them, but you still did what they asked. Tell them now to get ready for church and they just say, "I'm not going."'

This conversation is not startling in its revelations. Today, somewhere, a similar conversation will be playing out in a dozen coffee shops across the country as parents – and particularly mothers – travel the roller-coaster ride of raising a teen girl. The roller-coaster analogy is a good one. Remember the last time you took the plunge and fastened the seatbelt on a theme-park ride? At the start, your expectations are high: you can do this; it almost looks easy. But you find yourself holding your breath as the roller-coaster car chugs slowly up to an incredible height. Along the way, a fear begins to chill your bones. This could go either way. All of a sudden you don't feel as though you have what it takes, but it's too late to get off. You think of those headlines you saw once, about some cable car in some country, becoming stuck mid-ride. All of a sudden, that takes on enormous significance. The next time that happens could be any minute now. Then, as your car reaches the top, smiles kill the fear. You can see forever, over the hills and valleys and into the next district. Your car, far below, is a tiny speck in the car park. Everything is going to be okay. But that feeling is short-lived. Out of nowhere, the car takes off, fast and in a downward spiral. Faster and faster. The pace is furious as it reaches the first loop. And then another. And another. And another. You feel sick. Your stomach is churning. You want to get off, and you wonder how many more times you have to have your stomach turned inside out ... before the ride finally pulls up, safely.

Like the mothers in the coffee shop, most parents will know that a 14-year-old is wired to build loops around your day. The morning smiles and the frequent hugs that once greeted you morph into an eye-roll or an early-morning growl. The dress she loved when she persuaded you to buy it last week now looks 'so lame, it's really embarrassing'. And she's mortified that you will be wearing it to school. To *her* school! 'Do you have to do that?' she demands. Of course, you've worn it on purpose; your aim all along is to discombobulate her in front of her big circle of friends. While on the subject of school, why are you even involved, she might ask. No-one else's parents go to tuckshop. No-one else volunteers. It's naff. Sucking your breath in, you'll try to reassert your authority by asking her to wash up. There's a flood of tears, a tsunami of emotion that drowns everyone's mood in an instant. It might be the same response, later, when you ask whether she's completed her homework. On some days, you might even get the same response by asking her to spell her name. 'Why do you always pick on me?' she asks. And while we're on it, she doesn't want to continue the annual mother–daughter weekend away. She never did like it.

A day in the life of a parent can be exhausting and exhilarating in equal measure, and most parents might not be surprised to learn that in a survey of 2000 parents (mentioned in Chapter 1), 14-year-old girls were nominated as the most difficult. Conducted by thebabywebsite.com, the survey found two 'difficult' phases in a child's life, with the general consensus putting the teenage years above toddler tantrums. The site's co-editor, Kathryn Crawford, says while new parents feared the 'terrible twos', parents of teenagers will tell them the worst is yet to come. 'Ironically, many toddler traits surface again when children become teenagers, but often become even more difficult to deal with.' Parents find themselves lurching between frustration and defeat, wondering when the Addams Family stole the Brady Brunch factor from them. When did their opinions, so often parroted by their daughter, become so old-fangled that they were doddery? Thousands of dollars in cello lessons and she gives it up in a second. She no longer wants to sit in the front seat of the car; the back seat with earphones is where it's at. She'll agree to you following her on Instagram – but don't dare leave a comment!

She will be, often, her parent's toughest critic. 'They just don't understand. Anything,' Jocelyn, 14, says. 'Times have changed since they were 14 and we have a lot more pressure to do well in school and a lot more stress due to others' judgements,' says Peta. And Clara: 'My mum and dad can never admit that they're wrong. Literally ever.'

It's easy to sit in a glass house throwing stones, so I ask a big group of 14-year-olds to write down how they think they would parent their own 14-year-old daughter differently, down the track.

> *'Don't get really angry at your daughter. Try to understand and put your feet in her shoes.'* – VONNIE, 14

> *'Listen to me. Let me say exactly what I am feeling and allow me to say whatever I want.'* – FIONA, 14

> *'Advice to my parents: when your 14-year-old daughter is having a bad day, don't be too harsh on them.'* – ALEX, 14

> *'Be calm and stop getting so stressed.'* – JUSTINE, 14

Others suggest they would push their daughter to get a part-time job, study harder, take up karate, take dance lessons or learn a new musical instrument. The list goes on. But the three answers that stand out are: listen more, spend more time with them, and let them make their own mistakes. They yearn for encouragement – 'Be supportive and tell her she can be anything she wants' – and a closeness – 'I would want my relationship with my child to be a really close one'. Experts offer an easy solution here, saying parents need to step out of their world and join their daughters. Often they ask their daughters to join them in doing something of interest to adults, not teens. Turn that on its head, they say, and watch YouTube, or do something your daughter likes to spend time doing.

Liv, 14, is driven by her parents to study hard. But she says she misses them terribly. They're in the house physically, but she misses how it used to be: that relationship she had with her mum and dad a couple of years ago. She'd love to feel connected to them again, but doesn't know how. What really hurts, she told a counsellor, is when she sees movies showing family love. She wants that in her own life. It sounds schmaltzy, perhaps, but with more and more parents working, and more and more children granted overseas holidays and new computers and the latest phone, what these girls really yearn for is time. And that's not just confined to 14-year-olds. Repeatedly, in researching this book, parents told me about David Rosenman, the father from Minnesota, USA, who popped up on their Facebook accounts one morning after posting about his trip to the coffee shop with his nine-year-old daughter. 'She brought with her a little crocheting activity; I brought the newspaper, a notebook and pen, and my phone,' he posted. So far the story is extraordinary in its ordinariness. It was going to be a father–daughter date like those held every weekend at fast-food chains and coffee shops and parks. But on this day, David's daughter made a request. 'Daddy, can you not read the paper or doodle or check email today? Can we just be together?' David Rosenman posted their exchange online, privately at first, but it was later shared. Soon it had been published around the world, in 18 different languages. 'She showed me her yarn project,' related David. 'I recalled the day she was born. We compared notes about whether or not couples at other tables were on "dates". She told me about her friends and their hamsters. I watched her chew her breakfast sandwich and melted a little bit as I thought about how much I love her.'

When Rosenman returned from paying at the counter, he found a note, face-down, on the table. His daughter told him a lady had asked her whether he was her father, and told her the message was for him. He turned it over and read it:

'I work at a school where many daughters don't have fathers and those who do have never in their lives had him watch and listen and devote 100 per cent of his attention to her for as long as you did on one Sunday morning. You have no idea what a gift you are giving to all the teachers who are responsible for educating her from now until she graduates.'

David posted that on Facebook, saying, 'Please don't wait for your child or other loved one to plead for your attention like mine did.'[1]

The story gets better. I contacted David while writing this book, and he says that someone online recognised the handwriting in which the note was written and identified the teacher who wrote it. 'She then reached out to me and my family. We all returned to the coffee shop for a reunion meeting, and since have become friends. This year, I'm volunteering at the school where she teaches. Someday I hope our daughter will, too,' David says. He says the whole episode has served as a reminder to him that we have one precious life and that 'it can be so much better when we, fellow human beings, listen to, observe, and support one another'.

Alex Curtis, Kids Helpline Counselling Centre Supervisor, says the nub of the problem for teens can be simply that they want more time with their parents. Dad is busy at work; so is Mum. When they arrive home, there's dinner and bed. Downtime – sitting around the kitchen table chatting, or playing a board game – doesn't happen often. The conversation revolves around homework and chores, sporting timetables and early starts the next day. 'You know, from [my work] and being a mother, I believe the biggest thing I've learnt is the power of being there for your 14-year-old,' Curtis says. 'You cannot underestimate the power of being there and of love. A lot of people think young people just want everything. They want this; they want that; they want the latest phone. From what I see here, young people just want to be heard, they want to be loved, they want someone who is there for them. I would definitely say that is overwhelming.'

Youth health nurse Helene Hardy nods slowly when she hears Liv's story about missing her parents. She hears it over and over again. It's a disconnection, she says, between parents and teens. She says she will often ask a 14-year-old she is addressing about a problem whether she wants to tell her mother about it. 'They just shrug. They don't know,' Hardy says. And then Hardy asks the girl who she's closest to at home. 'They'll say Mum, or a sister. I'll say, "Can you have a chat with Mum?", and they'll say, "No, I couldn't talk to her about that." It's the new norm. None of them sit together for a meal. They come home and the girls go straight into their own room. But these girls just feel disconnected from their parents. They're in the same house but they are not connecting at all.' Social media becomes their life line.

If the teens and parents were on different sides, Hardy would captain the girls' team. 'Parenting has lapsed. We are letting our kids down a lot. I see it so much,' she says. Hardy has worked with parents try to re-establish a relationship with their teens. She says she sometimes sees that 'ah-ha!' moment when parents remember what they should be doing: parenting their child. She uses the analogy of 'elastics', a game often played in primary school. The relationship might be stretched. Times are tough. Walls have gone up. But it's elastic, and it can move back in. 'Parents have to learn to listen, and be present. I know how hard it is to be working and be a caregiver, but five minutes can mean so much.'

'My parents work a lot,' says Amy, who is 14. 'They start at 6.30 am and end at 5.30 pm, so we don't really get time to connect because I'm busy with sport and school too. My mum and I fight a lot and she thinks it's because we don't see each other much, and that's where my nan comes in. When Mum goes away for work, which is 70 per cent of the year, my nan comes to look after me, so I share a lot with her.'

Associate Professor Alan Ralph is head of training at Triple P Positive Parenting Program, a program that is now in 26 countries. Ralph says opportunities to talk are few because both parents and teens are so busy, and that makes listening even more important. 'I often get parents to think about this and say, if you were to sit down and work out how many minutes each week you and your teenager are in the same space, not busy doing something, how much would it add up to?' He estimates it would be no more than an hour. But the problem is that parents then often use that time to talk about a behavioural issue, or an unclean room. 'That exchange is usually not one that the teenager enjoys,' he says. 'So the strategy the teenager is likely to adopt is to reduce the opportunities for those type of exchanges.' Ralph suggests issues should be dealt with in a family meeting, held regularly, where everyone's voice can be heard. And don't use any casual opportunities to talk to your teenager to only pursue something negative. 'Use those opportunities for positive exchanges,' he says.

Just an aside here on family meetings. My husband suggested we hold them, each Sunday night, when our children were toddlers. To be honest, I didn't see the value – at least, not back then. We've kept up with the meetings, which we all take turns to chair. Each Sunday night we go through the minutes from the previous meeting, endorse them, and go on to general business. Now, a few years on, it's hilarious to read back over the old minutes and look at the issues that once focused our children's attention: the amount of ice-cream they received compared to their sibling, or their passionate objection to fruit in their lunchbox. Now it's the basis for planning family holidays and discussing everything from pocket money to parental work absences to friendship dramas. It's this type of meeting that Ralph recommends, when our children are teenagers. He says it provides a valuable forum where parents – and teenagers – can raise issues.

Susan McLean, former police officer and author of *Sexts, Texts & Selfies*, says slack parenting is no more evident than when it comes to dealing with social media. Parents could be tough in the real world, but not in the cyber world. 'I get sick and tired of it. If you're not somewhere you shouldn't be you can't have a problem. It's as basic as that when we're taking about technology.' In other words, don't allow your kids to access sites that pose dangers. McLean says she's been approached by parents saying she has no right to say her 10-year-old can't have Instagram; that it was a parental decision to allow access to it. McLean's voice rises. The terms and conditions set the age at 13, and parents needed to understand that. 'It's lying. No-one's going to prosecute a child but the problem is that if we allow children to believe it's okay to lie online – and parents go out of their way to help them – we're setting ourselves up for failure in the future. My argument is that it's just as easy to help your child to a good decision as it is to an honest one. We need parents to help kids. They are not capable of always making good decisions by themselves,' she says. Teen girls wanted, and needed, the parameters drawn for them. 'We either have the limp-lettuce parents who do nothing or we have the overbearing parents who say my child will never be on social media until they're 65. Neither option is the right one.' Principals support strongly the concept of giving your 14-year-old clear boundaries. Flo Kearney, former principal of Brisbane's Somerville House girls' school, says boundaries allowed teens to know when they've stepped over a line. 'I know there's a lot of research and philosophy and people's opinion about not giving them any boundaries – but in fact they thrive when they're given boundaries,' she says.

Julie Warwick, principal of a 1400-student co-educational high school at Robina on Queensland's Gold Coast, says sometimes the 'horse has already bolted'. 'If, as a parent, you are suddenly trying to equip your child with certain skills and you've left it until they're 14, it's going to be very difficult,' she says. Warwick, who is also a mother of a daughter, gives the example of parents who allowed their nine- and ten-year-old children to dress older than their age and wear make-up. It's cute then, but delivers a message that turns around and slaps them in the face when their daughter is 14.

Warwick, like many other principals, also sees parents too ready to jump in and solve problems for their daughters too quickly. This is something we don't do for our sons. 'By stepping back a little bit and letting them navigate their own dramas, you're actually doing them a favour,' Warwick says. 'You've got to be a role model around them; not buying in and becoming involved in all of their conflicts. Give advice, but also be prepared that it's going to be ignored.' Jane Danvers, principal of the Wilderness School in South Australia, says children must have the opportunity to fail and work it out for themselves. She talks not about self-esteem but self-efficacy. Girls needed to know how to set goals, deal with failure and reassess their plans.

Paul Dillon, Drug and Alcohol Research and Training Australia (DARTA) director, says that while teaching and parenting were two different roles, a middle ground applied when it came to making rules and boundaries.

'Ask your teen who their favourite teacher is and I can pretty well guarantee that it's not the one who tries to be their best friend,' he says. 'It's the one who starts the year off by making clear their expectations, outlining the rules that operate in their classroom and letting each and every student know why those rules exist.'

Jon Rouse, who heads Task Force Argos, says he often sees the well-to-do girls in high school lured into the most trouble. And he's quick to point the finger at parents. 'You have absent parents – very busy parents, and that's the world now – double-income [parents] working really hard to give their kids the best education they can ... but they're not there when their kids need them. That absence creates a number of social issues. If they're not getting the attention from Mum and Dad they'll go elsewhere to get the attention, and there's a lot of people ready to provide that attention. And sometimes it's just too late.'

In Australia, of coupled families, 21.7 per cent have both partners employed full-time, 3.7 per cent have both employed part-time and 21.4 per cent have one employed full-time and the other part-time.[2] The Wilderness School in South Australia mirrors those figures, with about 45 per cent of parents of students in middle school both working (full- or part-time). 'That looked very very different 20 years ago,' says the principal, Jane Danvers. From a female perspective, that's a good thing. Women should be able to choose whether they work outside the home. 'What we need to be doing is we need to be teaching our girls about how they actually navigate that pressure between their personal and professional lives,' Danvers says.

Dr Amanda Bell, principal of the University of Sydney's The Women's College, says there is another factor that sometimes surfaces as working parents try to provide their children with an education beyond what they might have had. She labels it 'competitive parenting', where a 'good mother' feels compelled to provide every opportunity for her daughter that she may not have had – ballet, netball, tutoring to get into extension classes, violin lessons. The list goes on. Increasingly there has been a trend, Dr Bell says, for women to take a year off work when their child enters Year 12, so that they can be there for them. 'What is that saying?' she asks.

And while the parent–child engagement might be put towards providing opportunities rather than time at the kitchen table, parents are also increasingly wanting a say in their children's education. Principals and teachers tell stories that border on the fanciful. But there are too many of them not to take note: parents, in hysterics, calling because a child should have got an extra half mark in an exam out of 80; or sending a legal letter after their child wasn't chosen for a leadership position over someone else; shopping for psychologists to give their child special consideration; buying all the sport equipment for a school on the proviso their daughter makes the team. It's endless.

One principal talks about a mother who 'nearly had to be hospitalised' after her daughter was devastated because her friendship group would not let her sit with them. 'You feel like saying, "Just trust your daughter. She'll be okay. Perhaps she doesn't belong in that group."' That principal, like other parents with daughters, has seen it happen with her own daughters. 'If I had let myself get heartbroken about that . . . I would have just aged myself. Our parents didn't lie awake looking at the ceiling at 2 am worried about a slight that some other girl might have made. Just trust your daughter. Trust her. Have faith in her. That's my message.'

That advice is mirrored by others – but author and teen expert Michelle Mitchell, who blogs at michellemitchell. org, also warns that teenagers will often put 'trust' out like a bargaining tool. 'Whenever teenagers [do that], I just say to parents, "take the trust issue completely off the table", because it's not really about trust. Your job is to protect them, not to trust them.' The girls, when asked, yearn to be trusted.

'Trust me more. Let me make my own mistakes and learn from them.'

'They don't trust me when I know I will make the right decision. They don't even give me a chance most of the time. When my mum and dad and I aren't in a bad

mood we get along, and that's when we have a good relationship.'

'[If I was a parent] I would be patient with them and trust them, unless I knew they were up to something. I would believe that the decisions they were making were the right ones unless I had proof they were making the wrong ones.'

'If I was a mother of a 14-year-old, I would trust my child, understand what they're going through – but I would set some rules.'

Mitchell makes this point, though: teens often want significantly more independence and freedom before they might have the cognitive or emotional maturity to deal with it. 'It's an age when it's very easy for parents to let go because teenagers are demanding they let go, but I think when parents let go too quickly there becomes this gap where kids become unprotected.' Parents need to assess the risks. 'Sure, trust them to walk across the road safely, do their homework, turn up to a part-time job, but I wouldn't trust them with decisions that are going to change the course of their life at that age. Some parents have said to me, "She's got a boyfriend. We really like him as a family. We let him stay over. We trust them. He does stay on the bedroom floor but we do trust that they're doing the right thing." Two months later there's a pregnancy test. It's really scaling that trust and assessing the risk. Sometimes parents give up their right to be able to say no because they feel obligated to extend that trust and it becomes like a bargaining tool. "Why won't you let me, Mum? Don't you trust me? I told you I won't do that again." It's about assessing the risk, and if the stakes are not high and the risks are not high I think it's incredibly important for our kids to fail.'

'At Mum's I can have the phone in my room. At Dad's I can't. He's like the strictest parent of all my friends. Sometimes I stay at Mum's for that reason.' That's Daisy, and it captures the view of many girls growing up in single-parent families. Most of them accept the break-up. Some struggle through puberty issues, particularly when they are staying at their father's home, but the issue of different rules is overriding: pocket money handed out at one parent's home and not at the other; a bed curfew at one and not the other; permission to go to parties at one and not the other. It confuses the teenager – particularly when it comes to how different parents treat the issue of social media. Single-parent homes also feature strongly in the work of Senior Constable Kelly Humphries and Detective Senior Sergeant Grant Ralston, but that's not the determining factor in teens going astray. What these two seasoned officers believe is that it comes down to three issues: is the parent supportive of their teen? Does the teen come from a stable environment at home? And how connected are the teens to the adults in their life?

These officers say that they can tell at an early age whether a young person is on track to re-offend. 'Fourteen is a big, big, big turning point in life,' Ralston says. 'What I come across as a police officer and as a detective is that 14 is that age where they are not a child anymore who wants to rely on Mum and Dad, they want their independence, but they're not mature enough to catch a train to the city and be confident enough not to talk to strangers and all of that. They're still in that very vulnerable stage; they're really on the border. They can go either way at that age. We think it's a really important age.'

Ralston and Humphries paint a picture of modelled behaviour: parents who dabble in drugs have children who dabble in drugs. If parents accept truancy, or poor sexual practices, or even glue-sniffing as part of 'growing up', it's akin to supporting it, and their teen will attract friends from a similar background. 'When you look at the families of the groups they hang with, they all seem to be similar. There may be an offender in that family. It's not always a broken family, but we do see that problem children do come from broken homes,' Humphries says. 'If the parent is broken and doesn't having the coping skills, then the kid doesn't have the coping skills because they don't have the behaviour model. But if the parent has gone through an issue and overcome that problem, then they are more likely to instil those skills in their child.' This is the case whether the child belongs to two loving parents, a single parent or another family type. 'If you've got a really good relationship with your parents from the beginning and it's consistent and you know you're supported – even if the family splits up – you're going to be better off than someone who doesn't have that support,' Humphries says. Ralston says there is another family type that is concerning to police. Here, the parent or parents provide the absolute basics, so they stay below the radar of authorities, but that's all. 'They might get basic food, but their parents are involved in criminal activity. Police can see how high the chances are that they will follow [down] the same road. We are really worried for those ones.'

And fathers play such a crucial role. Senior educator Flo Kearney says daughters often pull back from their fathers once they hit Year 9. 'They shut themselves off. Once they were all over their fathers, sitting on their laps. They're now much more private about things. The parents – both of them – can become such an enemy.' If Dad is the family's authority figure, that can simply make things harder. And daughters will also begin to butt up against their mothers, wanting to be different from them. Principals raised that repeatedly. Marise McConaghy of Strathcona Girls' Grammar School says one of the most empowering things a girl can have in her life is a father who believes in her. From studies of the influence of fathers on women who are successful, certain lesssons have emerged. 'A crucial one of these is that fathers should try to communicate inferentially, not just [have] high expectations that their daughters are competent and able to get the job done, but they also have an underlying high regard for their daughters and convey that they just like "hanging out" with them and listening and talking to them,' she says. It seems that in between the dad jokes, listening tops the attributes of a good father. McConaghy has actually given fathers a multiple choice test, which makes the point. Here are a couple of the questions.

Your Year 9 daughter has had a falling-out with her friends and she is crying, saying that no-one in the group likes her and she has nowhere to go as no-one in the year level likes her. Do you:

a. *Sit down and forensically question her on all that has been said and done, taking notes.*

b. *Listen and tell her that it is all very unfortunate and hard but you know that she will be able to work through this.*

c. *Phone the parents of the girls in the group and threaten to sue.*

d. *Phone the school and tell them it is their fault.*

e. *Go and open a bottle of red wine and hope for the best.*

Your daughter comments that she looks fat. Do you:

a. Say, 'Yes, I noticed that you'd put on weight.'
b. Say, 'You are beautiful.'
c. Pretend that you did not hear.
d. Let her mother manage it.

Repeatedly the girls will paint Dad as the disciplinarian, the distant provider or the larger-than-life comic who embarrasses her around her friends. Or he disappears under the radar, when it suits. Harper, 14, tells the story of dragging herself to breakfast one morning to find her mother standing at the kitchen bench. 'You're getting a bit fat,' her mother said, before dismissing her comment as a joke. Harper worried all day at school, pinching her cheeks and asking her friends if they agreed. That night, she asked her father. 'I don't know,' he said. 'Ask your mother.'

Another factor stood out, and girls raised this many times. Evie's comment highlights the concern:

'My dad doesn't let me go to the shops by myself but he tells stories of how he would go out by himself all the time. That's why I don't think he really understands anything.'

Girls don't see it as an issue of the world being safer when their father was that age; they see it as what's good for the goose isn't good for the gander, or that males can do things they cannot.

This book is directed towards girls and their mums. That's mainly because the girls talked more about their mums, and the influence they had, but also because most of the experts I talked to focused their attention on the mother–daughter relationship. That isn't to say men, and dads, aren't crucial in a teen girl's life. They are!

Jeffrey, who has an adult daughter as well as two teenage daughters, says he's seen the role of both parents change over time. 'With my first daughter, we had more control over what she was seeing and doing and hearing,' he says. 'She spent a lot of nights on the phone, but we could hear the conversation and we knew when she was using the phone. She had time limits, too.' He says the sheer choice open to teenagers now – from school subjects to sporting activities to cultural pursuits – makes parenting more complex. 'The good thing is they have a whole lot more paths to choose. And the difficult thing is that they have a whole lot more paths to choose! This can make guiding them a tough job.' He says there is also a bigger expectation – from schools especially – that parents be deeply involved in their teens' lives, in a way previous generations were not. 'My first daughter lived her teens in a world familiar to me. My younger daughters are growing up in a world that is not as familiar. When something broke, like a bike, I could fix it. That's not the case anymore.'

A final issue here relates to siblings, and where your 14-year-old daughter falls in the family. The firstborn is often the one handled with kid gloves. Parents jump in quickly to defend them; their younger siblings are often left to fight their own battles. The girls I interviewed have a different perspective. 'Don't forget to look at how your parents compare siblings from being the youngest,' Aleisha says. 'I have found that they are more over my shoulder and protective, always wanting to know what [I'm] doing. I guess it's just because, being the last child, my mum wants to make everything right for me.' Or Catherine, who offers this: 'Let your child make her own mistakes.' She says that if she has more than one child she'll treat them individually – including punishment. Associate Professor Alan Ralph says parents invariably put enormous effort into their first child, often seeking assistance with the slightest problem. The second child might not be subject to the same intervention, and then if a third child joins the family, the second – or middle – child might receive even less attention. 'And if the mother is invested in her children to a large extent, letting go of that third one can be a real problem,' he says. It's worth considering that, because Ralph says each of those different scenarios means the teen might travel a different path in the natural teen/parent separation journey.

Parenting is, and should be, difficult. The demands it throws up change along the way, as children learn to navigate their own path. Former principal of St Aidan's Girls' School in Brisbane Karen Spiller sees that often, with parents struggling to understand why one daughter is a handful and the other two are not. 'You have to work on them separately so they don't have an investment in being naughty and standing out,' she says. Often, she recommends loosening the boundaries on the hard-to-engage child. As parents we have boundaries around our little ones. They are tight when they are small, and we have to open them up as they grow, allowing them to cross the road, travel on the train and go to their first parties. 'We have to let those boundaries grow because that's the normal way in which young people learn, and the more we open up those boundaries the greater the opportunity for them to try and test and fail and learn and so on,' she says. But parents sometimes will let go of the boundaries completely, to keep their daughter happy, or in the case of the third child because the first two had no difficulties. Sometimes parents are dog-tired, too. 'You can't give up entirely, but you've got to let the boundaries go a bit and at some point you have to let the child have some degree of voice in some decisions that are really important to her.' That often has the effect of the child pulling back herself. 'As parents we want to help. We don't want to [remove] the boundaries entirely but we're really scared they're making poor decisions. But we have to allow them a voice and an agency,' Spiller says.

And you have to pick your time. 'It's about grabbing those little moments in the car,' Alex Curtis from Kids Helpline says. 'When you pull up at home and you're engaged in a conversation, rather than just jump out of the car and think, "I've got to go make dinner", it's about stopping and finishing that conversation. That's really important.'

And perhaps it's worth remembering how it used to be, too. Sure, take away social media, and the pressures of doing well at school, and friendship issues. Pushing the envelope is something every 14-year-old will want to do. One retired school principal told me how he noticed three missed calls from his daughter on his phone. He ducked out of a meeting and called her back. She sounded on the verge of tears. Her 14-year-old daughter Ruby – his granddaughter – would do nothing she asked, and she was at the end of her tether. 'I doubled over laughing,' he says. 'It brought back so many memories for me – and I told her that.' He wears a huge smile now, relaying that conversation. Time – with your daughter, and history – can be a wonderful friend.

Look at me

'*I'm fat and ugly.*'

TERESA,
14

'*Sometimes I wonder if I'm pretty enough.*'

CAITLIN,
14

Take a minute and flick through your Facebook page, and read the comments directed at your young daughters or those of your friends. 'How gorgeous.' 'You look so beautiful.' 'Wow, she's really pretty.' 'Stunning.' It's all complimentary; sweetness and light for the young girls who brighten up their parents' lives in ballet costumes and gymnastics uniforms. But it's very different to the same accolades posted about boys at the same age. 'Way to go, Johnny.' 'Go hard, Tom.' 'You beat the best of them, Harry.' The compliments are just as robust, and as parents we lap it up. But the girls are judged, even in the eyes of their Facebook family and friends, by how they look, the boys by the way they act.

It doesn't start and end with Facebook posts. Consider the efforts put into dress-up day at kindergarten, where a flood of pink fairies fills the sandpit alongside their male peers, dressed in board shorts. Or the amount of money spent on buying the 'perfect dress' for the school formal. Or even how differently our female and male television presenters are perceived. A few years ago, at a Melbourne Cup day lunch, a group of beautifully attired women paraded around a table laden with champagne and low-fat salads, so that their husbands could vote on the best dressed. As the winner, a professional who had ducked away from a high-pressure job for a champagne with her girlfriends, was announced Best Filly on the Field, the others applauded. It was a light moment in an afternoon spent amongst good friends. The women dressed up, and were judged by how they looked – not by each other, but by the men.

So why should we expect our 14-year-olds not to consider how they look as central to their success? Why would we be concerned when we witness tears erupt because the perfect eyeshadow palette, ordered in plenty of time online, didn't turn up in time for the school dance? Why do we lie awake, late at night, worrying that

Maggie or Heidi or Tyler skips breakfast and picks at her dinner, concerned she'll attract an extra kilogram? I put those questions to all sorts of experts: psychologists, teen counsellors, principals, teachers and parenting gurus, and the answer played out like a chorus to a popular song: we often model that behaviour, without even thinking. We pay for the dress that we know is a touch too short, desperate to please our daughter and keen to make sure she stands out at her semi-formal. We sit on the couch with our daughter while *The Bachelor*, or *Married at First Sight* or *The Seven Year Itch* plays out on the television. We know Sally or Susie or Stephanie or Stella had a biology exam today, so pop into the newsagent and get her the latest girlie magazines as a treat. Or as Dannielle Miller, co-founder and CEO of Enlighten Education, says, 'Often we've perhaps passively accepted all of this – and then bizarrely turn around and say, "Gee she's growing up too fast!"'

There's no doubt that sexualised images play a bigger role now than they did when we were 14. In the '80s Diana Ross was sending us 'Upside Down' and Michael Jackson told us about 'Billie Jean' and Queen warned us that 'Another One Bites the Dust'. For younger mums, who turned 14 in the '90s, it was Whitney Houston's 'I Will Always Love You', Sinéad O'Connor's 'Nothing Compares 2 U' and even Toni Braxton's 'Un-break My Heart' that had us singing into the bedroom mirror, our hairbrush a make-believe microphone. *Sex in the City* might have had us gossiping to our friends, but Samantha Jones and her 'one-nighters' was balanced by Miranda, the career lawyer, and Charlotte, an art dealer who believed in love, not sex. *Happy Days*, while years old, still filled our lounge rooms in the 1980s, along with *The Brady Bunch*, *The Partridge Family*, *The Simpsons* and, my personal favourite, *Friends*. Ask the 14-year-olds now and it's *Pretty Little Liars* that tops the pops. It too is about a group of friends, but in this case one of the gang dies and a year later the estranged friends begin receiving letters torturing them for mistakes they've made.

But more than television, it's the image of those we admire that has starkly changed between generations. Agnetha Fältskog and Anni-Frid Lyngstad were not just the female members of Swedish pop group ABBA. They were style icons, with their fresh faces, superb hair and trendsetting clothes. *Charlie's Angels* Sabrina Duncan (Kate Jackson), Jill Munroe (Farrah Fawcett) and Kelly Garrett (Jaclyn Smith) had the look many of us wanted. On my wall, they jumped out in tracksuits, their long hair parading down past their shoulders. Blonde, brunette and dark-haired, they were gutsy and tough and beautiful and adventurous. So why are the idols our own daughters aspire to so different? 'You and I would have had women whom we thought were beautiful, whom we aspired to be like, because that's a timeless phenomenon, but those women were relatively real,' Dannielle Miller says. 'I had posters in my room of ABBA and Charlie's Angels, and while they were genetically beautiful women and they would have had professional hair and make-up and maybe a bit of a wind machine, perhaps a soft lens, they were relatively human. The images today of women that the girls aspire to be like are airbrushed into being the impossibly perfect. And that's a completely different set of pressures. It means that these girls never look at an image of a woman that has not been manipulated in such a way that she's no longer really human.'

It's a point Indonesian supermodel Tracy Trinita made to a group of school girls in Brisbane last year. Trinita told the students she walked into a store in Indonesia to pick up a copy of *Her World*; she was gracing the cover. 'The newsagent guy was wondering why I was buying four [copies],' she says. She explained that she was on the cover, and one was for her mother, one was for her grandmother, one was for her aunt and she wanted to keep one herself. 'But when he looked at the cover and looked at me, he didn't have any expression – he didn't see any resemblance between me and the girl on the cover.' She said to the girls: 'Do you see me? Do you see the girl on the cover? Do we look alike? First, my face is chubbier in reality. My hair is thinner in reality. And I'm not as skinny as I am in the magazine. And this is the real me. Look at me.' She told the girls that every model wished she could look the way she looked in the magazine, but none of them did. Flo Kearney, the former principal of Somerville House in Brisbane, said Trinita's talk and her message – that girls should never measure themselves against someone from television or social media because it was not possible to look perfect – hit home with her students. But it's a message that needs to be reiterated. 'They hear it. They see it. Whether they take that onboard and actually absorb it into their self and their knowledge is the curious thing. We try to repeat the message; it's not about hearing it once. It's over and over again until it sinks in. When does reality set in? I'm not quite sure. But the more you can bring the real world to them, the better.'

Arun Abey, author of *How Much is Enough?*, says money is tied up with image, pointing to US research a few years back that showed a trillion dollars was spent annually on advertising. The teen demographic is smack-bang in the centre of the target audience. 'All of us – especially our kids – are being assaulted by a series of messages which says that intrinsic worth is not good enough,' he says. If we don't have the right watch, we're not quite good enough. Or the right hairstyle. If others at school have the handbag that everyone is talking about, we want it too. It's not just that we want it, it's the pathway to popularity. More people will like us if we do have that purse. We will get the right guy if our hair looks exactly like that.'

The end result is that many teens spend their days trying to be something they cannot be: impossibly thin, having perfect eyebrows and cheekbones that rarely exist outside photographs, and an athlete's legs. They need to look sexy because – in their minds and in the minds of their peers – that equals success. Size matters. Looks matter. Sultriness wins big points. Mia Freedman, the youngest editor of the Australian edition of *Cosmopolitan* and founder of popular website mamamia.com.au, says girls cannot escape that message. 'Our girls are growing up marinating in a society that values women for their appearance and their sexual desirability,' she says. 'You have to look hot when you're pregnant. You have to look hot immediately after having a baby. You have to look hot when you're young. You have to look hot when you're old. You have to look hot when you wake up in the morning.' That message is rammed home when you learn that the more revealing an Instagram photo is, the more 'likes' and comments it attracts. 'So you've got a generation of girls who are indexing their self-worth from the amount of likes they get on social media,' says Freedman.

Fran Reddan, principal of Mentone Girls' Grammar School in Victoria, says that girls are more sensitive to any comment about body image made by a male peer. 'When girls make a comment about body image they can brush that off,' Reddan says. 'But they take it more negatively when it comes from a boy.'

Dannielle Miller, in *Loveability*, the book she co-authored with Nina Funnell, says that girls (and women) are 'at war with our bodies because there is a war being waged on our bodies'. She continues, 'We get messages about what makes us beautiful and worthy of love from TV, the internet, the music we listen to and videos we watch, magazines, and the ads we see everywhere. We are constantly being told what we should look like, and the definition of beauty has become very narrow; it's all about being pretty, thin and hot.'[1] Ava, 14, makes Dannielle's point: 'I am not a small person. I am quite large, so body image and fitting in is hard.' So does Lucinda: 'If you are too small or too big it makes such a difference on how you feel – especially too small. I feel really left out of convos sometimes.'

Parenting expert Maggie Dent remembers, not too long ago, meeting with a big group of female students in a rural area. She asked them to jot down their thoughts about themselves on a piece of paper. 'I'm sitting in a room of about 45 gorgeous girls,' Dent says. 'I was staggered. The loathing, the self-disgust, the absolute hatred for parts of their bodies. I actually cried,' she says. The average age of the group was 14½ years. 'We had issues at times [when I was a teenager], but nothing was as intense as what today's girls are feeling.' Experts call it a perfect storm for this young generation – the flood of media and how young women are portrayed, the 24-hour social media cycle that doesn't allow them to escape, and an uneasy world where terrorism, and how it can unexpectedly unleash its hatred, sits at the back of a teen's mind. In days past, bombs could be going off in the next town and we wouldn't have heard about it. Dent says, 'They pick up all these things, and some have said to me, I don't know if I want to be in this world. We keep frightening children with the worst things about humanity and they don't see the good ones . . .' The girls take solace in what their friends think, and what people are telling them on Snapchat, and how many 'likes' they can conjure up. 'They actually tell me that if someone doesn't like their photo on Instagram, they have a shit day,' she says.

When children are young they'll wear what they like on non-uniform day, not what their friends suggest, and happily show it off to everyone. As puberty sets in, though, an obsession with appearance takes over for many girls. 'Given the major physical changes taking place in the adolescent body, it is perhaps no wonder that this is precisely the time when young people focus on and fret so much about their looks,' says school psychologist Jody Forbes, who is doing a university research masters degree in body image. 'More puzzling, perhaps, is that 42 per cent of teenage girls worry about their appearance compared to only 19 per cent of teenage boys.' In her research, Forbes found that body image was always one of the three top teen-girl concerns, and consequently girls had greater feelings of anxiety and depression, were more susceptible to eating disorders and had less confidence than their male peers. During my interviews, several girls tied their popularity to their appearance – 'I fear not being liked because of my body, appearance or personality,' Jenny told me – and fear of 'being fat' was even the driving force behind some girls participating in sport and dance, which they loathed. 'Some girls at dance don't like to dance, but if they don't they'll get really fat and stuff, but our dance teacher is really strict on it. If she doesn't see us eat then we're not allowed to dance,' Gabby says. And Cherry: 'Some people think if you don't do sport you'll get fat. That's why some play sport even when they don't want to.'

Forbes, like other experts, looks at the outside influences telling girls to worry about their body image, beginning with their parents – particularly mothers – asking, 'Does my bum look big in this?' or saying, 'I need to go on a diet', through to public policy officials who spend time focusing on the obesity problem in schools. This is a pertinent point made by Forbes, because most teen girls don't have a problem with obesity, they have a problem with body image. Forbes says there's also an economic argument behind the cost of low-esteem, pointing to a UK survey by personal care brand Dove which predicted that by 2050, lowered self-esteem could cost that country 14 per cent of its female managers, 16 per cent of its British female Olympic medallists and 17 per cent of female doctors and lawyers.[2] Talk to the girls, though, and they recognise the consequences; it's just the lure of wanting to look perfect is irresistible. 'Girls talk to me about it,' Forbes says. 'One girl told me how there was this mirror and she was doing her maths homework looking at what she was looking like. It's like when you're running you're thinking, what do I look like? So you start to see your own self as an object to be valued and evaluated.'

While the lives of 14-year-old girls seem to be filled with ironies, this raises another one. On the one hand they hate their bodies. They want to change their arms and legs and breasts and butts. They want thicker hair, a different pout. But on the other hand, and despite their anxiety about their bodies, they flood their social media accounts with half-naked photographs of themselves. Pouting by the pool in a string bikini. Flirting with the camera in the change room after netball. Dressed for the semi-formal, their top staying up with the force of good luck. They'll upload those photographs and watch them spread like wildfire, happy that they are being passed around and gaining 'likes'. And yet, they say they want to change almost everything about their bodies. Mia Freedman says that the irony can be explained, in part, by the fact that there is no message that tells us our appearance isn't the most important part of being female. 'And we internalise all of this,' she says. 'So even though we might know it logically and intellectually [. . .], it's not backed anywhere, by anything that you see. The people we see in public life who are considered successful and female are physically attractive, or altered,' she says. Mothers, and the roles they model, play a big part here, too. Freedman, in her mid-40s, says the idea of botox has crossed her mind sometimes. 'And then I think about what that will that say to my daughter if I do that. So I think we are looking at a generation of women – and I include myself in this (I get my nails done every week) – [who deliver the message that prizing their appearance is] the most normal thing in the world. Things like cosmetic surgery and botox and fillers are becoming really unremarkable – as unremarkable as dyeing your hair. So in many cases we can say one thing to our daughters but do something else ourselves, and what they really notice is what we do, not what we say.'

Low self-esteem often surfaces at this age because it strikes at the same time that girls are casting around to see who they want to be. And what they see reinforces the need to be thin, pretty and perfect. They see society rewarding *that* look. Photographs of celebrities filling their social media inboxes and plastering the sides of the buses they catch to school remind them of how life is better when you look good in a bikini. As Freedman points out, everything is telling them that to be an attractive, successful woman they need to be attractive to men, and therefore they need to look a particular way and behave a particular way. Of course most teen girls want to follow the latest fashions (which has taken us from velour tracksuits to wedges to jumpsuits). The surprise is not that they want to look the same, or that they want to look good, it's that 'good' is now defined as sexy, and that means thin, sleek and shiny hair, no pimples. It means looking like the digitally altered images of their online heroines. And this isn't possible – given that the average number of changes that are made to an online image of an already genetically gifted woman is about 40, says Dannielle Miller. Unbelieveable! 'So 40 things about her will be altered to make her impossibly perfect. That's a huge pressure,' she says.

Brisbane school principal Karen Spiller says it throws many girls into an enormous quandary. 'For some of them they're experimenting with behaviour that's very fringe behaviour in terms of their sexuality and they're not asserting anything of themselves because they don't yet know who they are.' They are compliant, willing to bend more than they should to fit in. 'The last thing the girls want to be accused of is that they are frigid. Being frigid is akin to having no friends because you're not attractive to boys, and frigid is very quickly linked to being lesbian – and that's just the language that will come out immediately,' she says. The girls, in so many ways, have this dichotomy thrust upon them: they want to be, and many of them see themselves as, leaders and academics. 'But at the same time they've got this incredible milieu where they have their own hormones popping and they can't manage that behaviour. They've got their own gradual interest in the opposite gender, and the push for that interest in that gender from their friends and friendship is everything. Besties are everything,' says Spiller. And that is reinforced day and night, via social media. 'When I was growing up, the phone would ring. Mum would say, "No, she's in bed ..." End of story. Even if you get the children to bring their phone out, there are so many devices in the home and it's so invasive that they don't have any downtime.' The girls recognise that. 'Back when our parents were kids, they probably had magazines with these pretty models and some billboards, but if you are on social media and the internet, it will pop up constantly,' Candy, 14, says. 'Every single day. The ads. The pictures on Instagram.'

There's another issue here, and that's the role of pornography. Many parents, when they were teenagers, might have found their friend's brother's copy of *Playboy* and stolen a sneaky look, and giggled. Now, if our daughters stumble across porn – which is more likely, given its ubiquitous online presence – the images of sex and sexual anatomy are entirely different. Women are hairless – nothing like the young women scouting around for perfection. That in itself is confusing. They've not had hair their whole life, have now got it as part of the changes at puberty, and the images being shown online are of women with no hair. The Australian Study of Health and

Relationships survey, which interviewed 20 094 men and women aged 16 to 69 in the year to November 2013, shows the increasing trend to shave, wax or laser pubic hair – with more than 75 per cent of 16- to 19-year-olds opting to do that in the previous year.[3]

Ask any doctor and they'll point to a lowered self-esteem being a factor in a host of other problems, including depression, anxiety, eating disorders and even self-harm, an increasingly significant issue in this cohort. In one group of 16 girls I spoke to, eight of them had not had breakfast that morning. And that's despite the queue of students who now turn up for the breakfasts put on by schools; the lines in some schools can run to hundreds of children. They're the ones who rushed out early that morning, or perhaps missed breakfast because of early sport. But ask those who have not participated in breakfast club and the reasons for them not having eaten are many: some didn't have time, others didn't feel hungry in the morning, and others admitted they did not consume breakfast because they were dieting. Helene Hardy, a youth health nurse, sees that unfold daily. 'They don't eat breakfast. That's my assessment,' she says. 'I ask them, what do you have for breakfast? About 20 per cent eat breakfast and every time I ask that question, they say they don't like breakfast. And this is across the age spectrum. Others don't like to eat in front of people so they won't have lunch, either.' This latter point surprised me. As a mother of younger girls, I've learnt the lunchbox etiquette: nothing unusual, nothing smelly. But at 14? 'Girls are aware of others making comments about their lunch – the smell of tuna, for example. You only pack that once.' Teachers point to a lower carbohydrate intake affecting the students' brains. 'They cannot learn,' one senior school leader says. 'We have conversations at our leadership table about girls who are in Year 7 and 8 and who might be really gun-academic. They'll lose a lot of body weight – they don't have an eating disorder, they're just not eating enough – and we actually see their academic performance slide quite dramatically, and we think they are inextricably linked. They are simply not getting enough protein and carbohydrates.' The need for nutrients, at this age, is crucial. Counsellors say they are seeing girls who have anaemia. Initially they present feeling tired or even depressed. Blood tests invariably reveal very low iron. 'Parents need to ensure girls are eating enough iron,' one student counsellor says. Another principal of a big girls' school says this: 'There are still girls who, while they don't have an eating disorder, don't eat enough. I think that pressure comes directly from their mothers. We know there's a link with anorexia with maternal lineage. In the richer suburbs around us, we see a lot of mothers who don't work, they go to the gym and they are very invested in their daughters being thin and gorgeous.'

That said, the number of cases of anorexia in this cohort is falling, according to principals, teachers, school nurses and teen psychologists. One principal with 20 years' experience as a school leader says she's seen a 'significant decline' in eating disorders in the past three years, compared to 10 or 15 years ago. 'Of course it's still there, but now we're seeing a lot more "cutting" than we saw 10 or 15 years ago. They've switched their pain management.' Helene Hardy confirms that self-harm has become a bigger problem. 'It's a control thing,' she says, shaking her head. 'I ask them why they are self-harming, in a really non-judgemental way. They pretty much always say they don't know. And if I ask them whether they want to stop, they will nod. They want to stop.' In our long conversation, over several cups of coffee, this is the first time Hardy falters. 'It's because they want to feel something. It breaks my heart. It really does.' Kids Helpline counsellors say the number of pleas for help, from teens who are self-harming, has been constant over the past few years; it takes up a big chunk of their counselling time. And Maggie Dent says it is now a common problem for parents to deal with. Compare the period 1985 to 1995, when Dent counselled students. She saw two or three girls who were self-harming in that entire decade. 'I'm seeing less resilient children who haven't been able to go out and have the bumps and the bruises and the fall-overs and [to] have to fend for themselves – not allowed to walk to school, not allowed to ride the bike . . .'

One mother told me how her daughter had asked if a friend could visit after school. Her mother welcomed the idea, knowing it meant her daughter was expanding her friendship group. 'Just don't bring up self-harm, Mum. She got bullied at her last school, so she cuts a lot. She'll hide it under her skirt, but just don't say anything if you see it when we get out of the pool, okay?' This mother had never raised the issue with her daughter, who was still 13. And yet the teen spoke about it in the same tone she would talk about her homework assignment. 'They become so secret,' another mother told me. 'Alison had a friend in her home room who was self-harming. She was doing it under her uniform. It amazed me that her parents didn't know about it but [that] half the class did.' This mother was in a quandary. Should she inform the parents? 'I've been told before it's interfering if you go to another parent,' she says. Right or wrong, that's the view of many parents. 'So at the end of the day I told my daughter to talk to her and suggest she go to the school counsellor. But I found it really hard – I was kind of lost on where to go, what to say.'

My older brother, Garry King, is an expert in this area, and runs Working with Young People Who Self-Injure workshops around Australia. A school counsellor, he says there are many reasons why young people are now self-injuring. Most teens don't do it to seek attention. 'The majority are involved in self-injury as a maladaptive coping strategy,' he says. 'A lack of resilience, combined with a lack of emotion regulation skills, puts many young people at risk.' He says research suggests up to 30 per cent of girls – from the time they commence high school through to their graduation – will self-injure, but the age when girls start was falling. King points to the fact that over the past four years, primary school staff attended 90 of the 94 workshops he's run. He says while research shows that half of those who self-injure will do so less than four times, it was important to focus on the motivation, not the injury. 'Linking young people to professional help is extremely important,' he says.

The pursuit of Little Miss Perfect – where girls need to look gorgeous, run like the wind, claim the debating trophy and the Maths prize – is creating a cohort of 14-year-olds, who are finding it hard to live up to expectations – their own, and others'. No-one wants their daughter to fail, at anything, and that might just be setting her up to fail spectacularly later. School leaders, in providing advice to parents on the issue, are in unison. 'Let your daughters fail,' says Dr Nicole Archard, principal of Loreto College in Marryatville in South Australia. Archard has studied girls, education and leadership for many years. 'Let them sort out their problems. Don't intervene too quickly for them,' she says. 'Don't give them a mindset that there are things they can do or can't do, or that they need protecting; that they have a problem at school so you'll come in and solve that problem.' Dr Maree Herrett, from Santa Sabina College in Strathfield, Sydney, agrees. And what words of advice would she give to a 14-year-old? 'Be brave, not perfect,' she says.

Caroline Paul, the author of *The Gutsy Girl: Escapades for Your Life of Epic Adventure,* believes we've coupled fear and femininity and need to decouple them. Mirroring the view of some educational leaders, Paul says that girls' self-esteem is tied up in outer values when we should be teaching them inner values. 'We teach them as girls to rely on other people's assessments of what they can do, and rely on other people's help – and of course by the time they are teenagers they are not going to be valuing their own inner strength because nobody's told them they have it.'

Sound byte saturation

*'People judge you and you become a lot more sensitive
to your body image and start trying new things.'*

IMOGEN,
14

Rihanna's song 'S&M' is blaring out of car radios the
length of the school drop-off queue. No-one is really
listening to the lyrics. It's the tune that draws them in.
But the lyrics are about sex and bondage.

The same song played centre stage at an international
police summit on abduction last year. Experts from across
the globe had gathered on Queensland's Gold Coast for the
Youth, Technology and Virtual Communities Conference
hosted by Task Force Argos, the elite Australian squad
that probes online sex offences. Detective Senior Sergeant

Grant Ralston was a delegate, and as the song started up, he recognised it immediately.

The next part, he says, he remembers in slow motion. Author and medico Dr Sharon Watkins Cooper, who specialises in developmental and forensic paediatrics in the United States, came to the stage. Ralston had been looking forward to her presentation; and she was now playing the video that goes along with Rihanna's song.

The room lit up. Rihanna filled the screen, in latex, sucking a banana, wearing bondage gear and simulating sex. Others in the video were tied up, their mouths bound with black tape, as whips and chains become part of her story. Sharon Watkins Cooper is used to the effect the video has on those who have never seen it. 'Of course, many ... are unaware of the significance of these seemingly on-the-edge lyrics ... until they see the video, which shows people bound and gagged, duct tape over their mouths at times, Rihanna with plastic wrap over her face and body, and other graphic scenes of sadomasochism,' she says.

Ralston, who is also the father of two teenage boys, looked down the row of seats at his colleagues. They all wore the same expression: horror. 'It's a really popular song. It's a really catchy song,' he says. 'It's in our discos. But when you see the video, you're horrified.'

For many decades, popular culture has consumed each young generation. The Beatles influenced the music choice of baby boomers the world over. Swedish pop band ABBA filled my teenage scrap books. Agnetha, Björn, Benny and Anni-Frid would stare out of every page, in different poses, 'Ring, Ring, Why Don't You Give Me a Call' in my head. As pitiful as it now sounds, I genuinely thought I was going to look like Anni-Frid, once my parents allowed me to use hair dye. Marrying Benny Andersson was in my distant future. Mamma mia, he'd find me irresistible! On other days, history class would be spent day dreaming. There, in some faraway land, I'd have hair like Farrah Fawcett and look like Kate Jackson – a mix of my two favourite Charlie's Angels. With my best buddies Monica and Julie, I'd be bullet-proof and famous.

So why is it any different today for a 14-year-old wrapped up in the lyrics of Halsey or Justin Bieber or Katy Perry, Fifth Harmony, Taylor Swift or Rihanna? I put that question to every expert along the way, and the answer is the same. It's because popular culture – unlike when we were young – now hangs as wallpaper in our children's lives. Music. Online games. Television. Movies. Concerts. Access means it's constant; there's no downtime and its influence is pervasive in colouring our teens' ideas, how they talk, what they wear and how they spend their time. The principal of one big public high school says it 'drenches' students, particularly girls, from a young age. 'Maybe it was the same when I was 14 ... but I don't think so. It's just so sexualised now. It's phenomenal.' She says she often wonders how her 12-year-old daughter knows the words of every song that plays on the radio. 'How does she even know who the Jonas Brothers are?'

Susan McLean, a former police officer and one of Australia's foremost authorities on cyber safety, agrees. 'One thing that has changed is that I don't remember wanting to always look sexy. Apart from Taylor Swift – who is not overtly sexual in what she posts – I can't name a celebrity, pseudo-celebrity or anyone in between who does not trade on their looks and their overt sexuality.' Not long ago, McLean was addressing 15-year-old school students when one of them raised their hand to ask a question. 'Susan, I still don't know why I shouldn't be sharing naked photos,' the girl said. The student went on to explain that Miley Cyrus regularly posted photographs of herself in skimpy clothing and nothing bad had befallen her, so why would it be different for this student? McLean said comments like that showed the disconnect between fantasy and reality. 'It's so easy for them to believe what they're seeing online, and if they see it enough, they're going to believe it's true.'

Ask a 14-year-old girl and she'll tell you there is a massive chasm between how *they* see popular culture and its influence, and how their parents – particularly their mothers – see it. While a handful will say, 'Mum understands being 14 because she was 14 too,' most of them will point to the differences that exist. Fourteen-year-old

Claudia says of her parents: 'Although they were 14-year-olds, time has changed. There are now phones and social media. They try to "protect" me but I know what is going on with the media. Sometimes they give me good advice but most of it is about heartbreak. Social media has changed the way things are.' Claudia's comments are replicated by her peers across the country. This generation of teens sees technology and what it provides them with as the big divider between their adolescence and the adolescence of their parents. 'Of course her life was different. She didn't have the internet,' Miriam says. And Grace says, 'They didn't have social media and there weren't as many expectations.' Things are now faster, more global, better connected. 'Even transport is different,' says Stella. 'Access is much easier now. Mum had to travel for 90 minutes to get to school.' Some of them even wish that life was a bit more like what it was for their parents. 'I wish it was the same and I could socialise more and ride bikes to houses like in the '90s,' Bridie says. By and large, however, the girls I spoke to believed the world had left their parents behind.

One co-educational public school principal I spoke to believes the impact of popular culture is far stronger on girls than it is on boys. 'You can see it, as you walk around the school. Fourteen-year-old boys are not as conscious of their appearance or what they are wearing. With the girls, you can see the amount of time they've spent on doing their hair. How you look is far more important to a 14-year-old girl,' she says. Talk to the girls and they agree. 'It's so expected to have a big chest, big bum, tan, [be] hot,' Tanya explains, 'and then the girls that aren't all of those things feel like crap and have no chance with anyone they could ever like.'

A 14-year-old's identity – who they want to be – is at the heart of popular culture. It's the time when they are working out their social self, their family identity, discovering independence and exploring who they might be down the track. In their parents' day, a teen's sphere of influence revolved mainly around their local school, their family and perhaps their sports field. Their communities were fixed, with few blurry edges. Now their social networks reach across the globe. They are cross-generational, too. Jane Danvers runs the Wilderness School in Adelaide. It is an independent, non-denominational Christian day and boarding school, catering for students from early learning to Year 12. Danvers terms technology an 'amazing enabler' that has allowed strong collaborative networks to grow for teenagers. But it also means, she says, that girls are living in a world that is not like the adult world of those who guide them. Theirs is a mishmash, where they feel empowered by feminism but face constant conflicts. 'My girls are incredibly driven, but they're also incredibly socially conscious,' she says. Globally aware, they are desperate for a better world; but they are also surrounded by identities like American TV star Kim Kardashian, who tried to break the internet by balancing a champagne glass on her famous derrière, and *Geordie Shore*, an MTV reality TV show featuring a group of friends living together, the plots thick with drunken antics, blazing rows and X-rated sex scenes. 'They are processing a huge amount of mixed messages in that desire to build their own leadership identity,' Danvers says. She identifies one of the biggest issues facing educators as being the need to provide the right environment – where children have opportunities to thrive, focus on their physical and mental wellbeing, and to be skeptical. 'It's no longer knowing about stuff,' Danvers says. 'It's about knowing what to do when you don't know, and how you navigate that.'

The girls nominate their favourite television shows as *Pretty Little Liars*, an American teen drama mystery-thriller television series; *Modern Family*, a comedy about modern family life; and *Friends,* about a group of young adults living in the heart of New York City. Also featuring strongly were *Gossip Girl,* about a blogger who ruthlessly reveals secrets about teens in upper-east side New York; and *Married at First Sight*, where singles agree to marry a complete stranger. No surprises there – indeed, many of these girls' mothers were also fans of *Friends*. But the medium of watching shows has changed. In my sample of 192 teens, only a few watched the shows in real time. Mostly they were screened, when the girls had time (which was often late at night, in bed), on Netflix, or downloaded onto their smartphones. That highlighted something else, too: the girls in this survey read books only occasionally. Sure, some labelled themselves avid readers, but for the main part this sample group focused on reading what was required for school. There wasn't enough time for anything else.

If entertainment acts as the backdrop to teens' lives, clothing and fashion are its central focus. And this – partlicularly sexualised and gender-stereotyped clothing – is probably a bigger area of concern for parents than what their kids are listening to or watching. Hosting a radio show for many years, I was regularly inundated with parents wanting to discuss this topic: toy stores that tried to influence five-year-old girls with bad-ass dolls wearing skimpy leather skirts and thigh-high boots; crop tops or mini bras for seven-year-old girls. While the focus is on girls' clothes, boys in this generation face the same pressure. 'My son loves that sport stuff. He's got to have it,' one dad says. His son is as tied up in fashion and how his mates will see him as any daughter. 'It's got to be the latest. And it drives popularity. That's very big for a 14-year-old. It's all about being popular. How many "likes" they have on social media.'

Inquiries or reviews into sexualised clothing have been held around the globe, and the consensus is that it's not a good thing. The American Psychological Association Task

Force on the Sexualization of Girls[1] is an enlightening read. It takes aim at five-year-old girls wearing fake teeth, hair extensions and make-up before being 'encouraged to flirt onstage by batting their long, false eyelashes'. It points to prime-time television, where teens watch fashion shows in which models are 'made to resemble little girls wear[ing] sexy lingerie'. Everyone – parents, child advocacy groups and psychologists – are alarmed at the trend, pointing to the harm it can cause girls as they navigate their way through teenhood. Indeed, research links sexualisation with three of the most common mental health problems faced by girls: eating disorders, low self-esteem and depression.

That makes sense. Think of the last school dance or party your 14-year-old attended. Many girls' identities are tied to the clothing they choose, and clothing for this age group increasingly highlights their sexuality. It's not new – remember a 15-year-old Brooke Shields telling us that 'nothing comes between me and my Calvins'? – but now it's all-pervasive, in part because of media that operates 24/7 and delivered straight into the girls' inboxes.

Advertising that directs its attention to the teen and younger accounts for a big difference between generational expectations. Children are now consumers. In-your-face advertising is now the backdrop on billboards passed on their way to school, in shop windows, during ad breaks on television, and with pop-up messages on social media.

Then there are music videos, websites, magazines . . . And the pseudo-pornographic nature of the imagery on show now is of deep concern, a point made by a landmark UK report titled Letting Children be Children.[2] It talked about what commentators call the 'pornification' of society – 'the blurring of boundaries between pornography and the mainstream'. It found nearly nine out of ten parents surveyed agreed that children were under pressure to grow up too quickly. 'This pressure on children to grow up takes two different but related forms: the pressure to take part in a sexualised life before they are ready to do so; and the commercial pressure to consume the vast range of goods and services that are available to children and young people of all ages.'

The bottom line is that it is not going away. Despite attempts at regulation – and Australia has been acknowledged as a leader in advertising regulations targeting children – it is impossible to border-control the marketing that spams our teen girls at every point. And it adds to a popular culture landscape that moulds our girls' views on everything from drugs to marriage.

So what can parents, or teachers, do when it's apparent that a sexualised culture umbrellas our teens? How do we act when regulation, in those domains where it has been tried, has not been able to pull up social media, and where the profits of business and media can rest on the lure of that same culture? I asked that question over and over – to every principal I interviewed, to every teacher, to every parent. And there was a uniformity of opinion: it cannot be stopped. Nor is it reasonable to stop it. What is important is twofold: first, for the girls to learn to think critically, which will allow them to separate the good from the bad; and secondly, to make critical-thinking skills a priority in what they are taught. That second point is important, because currently that is not the case – at least, not in most homes. Ask any parent the priority they have today for their 14-year-old daughter and 'critical thinking' doesn't feature once. The list is long: to get on with her friends at school, to forget her violin less, to do well in her science test, to choose wisely at tuckshop, to make the basketball team, to eat all her lunch, to grow up into a strong, independent woman. It goes on, and all of those might be important, crucial even. But each day, teenagers are confronted with decisions – and that ability to decode the message and make a sound judgement is paramount.

Some countries have tried an interesting approach. Take South Korea for example. Faced with a generation of teenagers addicted to video games, the Ministry of Culture, Sports and Tourism acted. It introduced a law, dubbed the Cinderella Law, which limited teens playing online games. Under the law, players under 16 were blocked between midnight and 6 am. (Teens soon began attempting to circumvent the ban by connecting to servers outside South Korea, or accessing the games via their parents' identification.) Last year, Ethiopian officials took a similar tack. They blocked social media sites – including Facebook and other mobile apps – across the country until its 254000 students had completed the national school exams.

The success of such measures is limited – and this generation, more than any other, will sneak around the rules because of their technical prowess. So the best thing to do, surely, is to equip them with the resources to survive. 'We can't lock our girls in towers but we can educate them and give them the skills to critique culture,' author and educator Dannielle Miller says. Those skills should include understanding marketing messages and agendas, being able to deconstruct images to see when they have been manipulated, and having a solid foundation in understanding feminism and gender equality. 'At the age of 14, they are very much on the radar for the beauty industry and the diet industry and the fashion industry. They will be targeted in terms of advertising,' Miller says. 'And they are being asked to deal with some pretty adult issues and choices – but they still might only have quite childlike strategies to fall back on.' She loves to teach girls to unpack the messages aimed at them. 'It's one of those illuminating moments when you can almost see the light bulb go on – when they start to deconstruct what they see around them and what's presented to them. [They] start to see everything around them a little bit differently and are more discriminating.'

Jane Danvers says the filters through which girls read, and how they reframe content in relation to themselves, is important. She raises the issue that the girls will raise with me in focus groups, over and over – the number of followers they have on Instagram. Three hundred. Four hundred. Four hundred and sixty. And the most in this group of 192 girls? 'More than 1000,' Rachel says. How does a 14-year-old know 1000 people? And taking the advice of experts that you only 'friend' someone you would welcome at your home, would Rachel have 1000 friends she would be happy – or be allowed to – 'hang out' with? When questioned, the girls mainly admit they don't know that many people. 'But they know people who know me, so it's fine,' says Rachel. But is it? And what about the fabulous irony in strong, independent girls judging their own popularity by the number of 'likes' they attain on social media? Certainly, our teen girls believe they gain social capital in their friendship groups through their social media activity – and you can't help but think that is a driving factor to the number and types of photographs they are uploading. 'This is a world that we're trying to understand,' Danvers says. Understanding – and dealing with this issue – has become part and parcel of the girls' school days for educators. But parents have a key role here, too, and together educators and parents need to build a capacity for girls to filter the messages they receive and to boast a strong self-efficacy. That's the advice of the experts.

That 'F' word – feminism – strikes an interesting response when raised amongst the 192 girls I interviewed. In short, it stinks, demonised by the media and reminiscent of these girls' mothers and their fight for equality. But it's important – and reassuring – to know that it is the word, not the sentiment, that they don't identify with. Take these comments as examples:

'I'm not a feminist. Why would I be? I can do whatever Iike.'

'I'm not but my mother is. She goes on about it. I know I'm equal to boys.'

In Dannielle Miller's research, only about 10 per cent of female students identify as feminists when asked. 'I think they *are* feminists when you explain to them what feminism means,' she says. 'By the time we explain what it really means, and the issues important to feminists, 100 per cent will say yes, and it will be like "Amen, Sister!" and they'll be high-fiving. They'll be right onboard.'

Regardless of whether they label themselves with the tag of 'feminist', Mia Freedman says the girls are genuinely seeing the world through a feminist lens, possibly for the first time. She points to the 2016 Olympic coverage, which raised issues of sexism, and the blanket media coverage of Big Bash star Chris Gayle's treatment of a female sports reporter during a television interview in May 2016. 'Suddenly there were all these conversations about why it wasn't appropriate for him to be flirty with a female reporter, and that was the main topic of news for over a week. That's fantastic,' she says. 'I always cheer when things like that happen. It's a massive change: it's called out; it's got a name; it's being discussed and a light's shining on it. And I think that's an incredibly positive thing.'

Miller is passionate about how we talk to 14-year-olds about popular culture, saying that parents should remember that same passion they had for their teen idols. 'What's really important to keep in perspective is that so many young girls are doing really well,' she says. When Miller's daughter was 14, One Direction ruled her world, passionately. 'I often say to parents that the key to all of that is to not demonise [their passions] and to realise that that's a really important part of their development. It's something we all experienced. Beatle-mania, Charlie's Angels and ABBA . . . and there's something quite beautiful about it – that shared deep love that only a 14-year-old, almost, can feel for things. Their level of passion for things they are interested in is astronomical.' That's borne out in other ways. Ask high school students to volunteer for a Clean Up Australia Day, or to visit the elderly, or to wrap

Christmas presents for the poor; often it is that group of passionate 14-year-olds, with love to burn, who will put their hands up. In part that's the brain working – it gets wired up for social connectivity. 'When you meet a 14-year-old and ask her to tell you why she loves Harry Potter so much, her whole face will light up and she'll gush and gush and be so passionate about it. I think it's sad in a sense that we lose some of our passion for things as we get older,' Miller says.

Since the 1970s, education has continually been reformed around the globe with the aim of improving female participation. But the results, by any standard, are not worth boasting about – at least not yet. Dr Nicole Archard, principal of Loreto College in Marryatville, South Australia, has also been dean of academic studies at Wenona School in North Sydney. Archard's passion for girls' education is mirrored in her degrees, which include Bachelor and Master of Arts, Diploma of Education, Master of Educational Leadership, Master of Theological Studies, and Doctor of Philosophy, focused on girls' education, women and leadership. This is what she says in relation to the education reform that's been unfolding for decades: 'In the 40 years since that's happened, it has had very little impact on girls taking up subjects which are still "boy" subjects.' She gives the subject of physics as an example. Of the HSC students studying physics in New South Wales, 80 per cent were boys and 20 per cent were girls. 'We can't say that in the last 40 years we've been successful in making outcomes different for girls.'

Popular culture is a better determinant of what our girls become. And according to every expert you speak to, it is still delivering a gendered understanding of what girls are and what they should be, how they should look, how they should speak and how they should act. Archard says girls need to understand themselves, and believe in themselves. 'It's not just providing them with role models and developing the skills. They've got to have that internal belief that they belong, that they can fit in and that they have the capacity to do things,' she says. While boys were more likely to show confidence and a greater belief in being able to do something (even if they couldn't), girls were more worried about how their peers would judge them. 'That then becomes a barrier to "I will put my hand up" or "I will speak out" or "I will take action" or "I will do something different to my friends". They're much more worried about peer feedback and influence and social standing,' she says. That makes sense. Boys tend to outwardly demonstrate their frustrations or anxieties, but girls are good at hiding it – or, in the words of Miller, putting on a 'perfect girl facade'. 'They may be performing academically, they may be doing well in terms of sport, they may even seem to have some strong friendships – but often it is only those closest to them, like their parents, who will have an insight into how much is happening below the surface,' Miller says. 'Those same girls may be struggling with self-doubt, with anxiety, with depression, with eating, and feeling huge pressure to perform and keep up that perfect girl facade. And it's something that's really celebrated in popular culture, too, through Instagram and social media accounts that only show the glossy, happy, successful side of life. It's important to keep in mind that even girls who look like they're doing very well still very much need and deserve support.' So how do you know whether your daughter needs help, or not?

Little Miss Anxious

'I'm scared that I won't succeed or be happy.'

MOLLY,

14

Molly, this chapter is for you. It doesn't matter what school Molly attends. It doesn't matter what state, either. Because Molly could be Claire, who is in another state, or Grace or Kylie, who live in another part of Australia. They want to talk about anxiety, but just not publicly. It's their secret, even from their friends, and they don't feel normal. Across Australia, I asked girls to write on a scrap of paper something they'd really value their parents understanding; the issue we might not have addressed in any interviews but that was important to them. After we talked, I gathered up the pieces of paper, and saw the word 'anxiety' pop up, time and time again. 'Please don't forget that mental health is important. Stress.

Anxiety. Depression,' Tara wrote. 'Please look into insecurities and mental health issues. Sometimes I feel so sad I don't know if it's normal,' Madeline wrote, adding that she'd also like to learn self-acceptance. And India, explaining how she feels as though she wears anxiety as a big overcoat daily, wrote this: 'I don't know what I want to do after school. I wish people would stop asking me. I have no clue and don't like thinking about it because I feel like I'll end up on the streets and not in uni.'

When 14-year-old girls are asked the reason they think they're anxious, several factors arise, but when pushed to pick one, the most common answers were the future, abandonment, something happening to their parents, and failing. 'People abandoning me,' Rose said. 'That I won't succeed or be happy,' Eloise wrote. 'Failing an exam and not being able to get into a good uni or job and being able to support my future family,' Annabelle said. 'I'm scared of finishing school and not being able to do what I want or being successful with what I do,' said Lauren. And the other big issue, which surfaced in every group of girls I met, was death. 'Dying.' 'Dying alone.' 'Death of a loved one.' 'Homicide.' 'The inevitability of death.' 'Death.' 'Losing my parents.' 'Losing people I care about.'

Indeed, so common was the fear of death, at this age, that I raised it with psychologists and educators the nation over. And their view? It was not only common, it was normal. Dr Amanda Bell, principal of The Women's

College at the University of Sydney, and formerly principal of Brisbane Girls' Grammar School and an art teacher, says that it was never unusual that the works presented by students of this age, or even a bit older, were underpinned by a gothic theme – 'a preoccupation with the darker side of humanity'. 'It's through my art teaching that I'd think, "Yes, this is just part of the way they explore what a more difficult part of life is and come to an awareness of that"', she says. The girls, at 14, are seeing their place in the world, and value their parents' role, even when they don't show it. They've learnt that life doesn't go on forever, through the death of a grandparent or someone similar. Perhaps a friend in their class has had a mother or father die of cancer, and it all becomes vivid. Death is real. So is life. Fran Reddan, from Victoria's Mentone Girls' Grammar School, says the teens are responding to a more fearful community and the constant barrage of bad news. They tell her they are wary of someone who might hassle them on public transport, or of the possible dangers in taking the dog for a walk when the sky is turning dark.

Clinical psychologist and author Andrew Fuller says the fear that can take hold of teens is nothing new, and he goes on to chart the external influences that might have had the same impact on their mothers or big sisters. Back in the 1980s, adolescents sweated through the night over Freddy Krueger, the serial killer who slaughtered his victims in their dreams in *A Nightmare on Elm Street*. The 2005 London bombings, which saw the deaths of more than 50 people at the hands of terrorists, left a queue of girls with nightmares and new fears. World events, and now particularly the unpredictability of terrorism, has left an indelible mark. 'Because of the vivid emotionality of teenagers, they're more vulnerable to picking up those toxins in our society,' Fuller says. He explains an exercise he puts to a group of female school students, where he asks them to imagine walking along a dark alley one night, and hearing footsteps. 'Many of them have no idea of what they would do – yet it is a fear that they've thought about,' he says. They've never formulated a plan to deal with the scenario, however unlikely it might be. 'The point there is that they have a sense of fear and don't know what to do with the fear.' Fuller is a strong advocate of empowering and mobilising girls to solve problems. 'If we want innovative, creative, problem-solving young women, we have to give them opportunities to solve real-world problems to cut their teeth on.' It has to be real and it has to be practical – like donating shoes to Africa, or helping out in an aged-care facility around the corner, or turning up for a shift at a homeless shelter. In fact, the Year 9 camps, or off-campus schooling, that has been discussed elsewhere in this book tries to capture some of that real-world 'doing' that Fuller talks about.

The girls talk about anxiety like it is a big shadow appearing at their bedroom window. They know there might not be a real basis for it but they don't really want to tell anyone about it, perhaps for fear that it becomes true. Leonard Sax, an American psychologist and author, wrote an article for the *New York Times* describing 'the laid-back, underachieving boy; the hyper-achieving anxious girl'.[1] He says that in his practice over the past decade he has observed an increasingly common pattern. In one case, his patient's parents were concerned about their 16-year-old son: he was not working at school and his grades were slipping. He spent his free time online, and was as 'happy as a clam'. Both parents were actually quite proud of their 14-year-old daughter, who was a straight-A student, an athlete and had many friends. Dr Sax says that when he met her she revealed she wasn't sleeping properly. She suffered a shortness of breath, and had begun cutting herself with razor blades. 'On the surface, she is the golden girl,' he wrote. 'Inside, she is falling apart.'

Studies show that 54 per cent of girls suffer an episode of depression or anxiety during their teens; that's almost double the percentage of boys (29 per cent).[2] Fuller sees it often, and says 26 per cent of girls in Years 9 and 10 have significant psychological issues to deal with, often centring around an inability to concentrate or sleep, and anxiety. And here's the twist. Often it's the highly accomplished students – those in extension class, and wearing the class captain or student council badges – who are suffering. Two years ago, when visiting a specialist, I noticed psychiatrists' waiting rooms next door packed with girls, aged about 16, all in school uniform. 'I'm seeing it every day,' my specialist said. The girls were being treated for anxiety. Fuller sees the problem develop a couple of years before these girls celebrate their 14th birthdays. They don't feel 'empowered' as 10- and 11-year-olds, and as compliant, good students they don't learn to shift gears as they travel through Years 7 and 8 and into the later years of high school. 'That's very tough. Some will be very successful. But others think, "Hang on, I've been a success all the way through, thank you very much. What's going on here?"' and they blame themselves,' he says.

It's the warmth in her voice that first strikes me about Kim Kiepe, former principal at St Hilda's Anglican School for Girls in Perth, and now Brisbane principal at Somerville House. She's in charge of 1250 girls. While boys are students at an infant level at St Hilda's, it becomes an all-girls' school in pre-primary. Kiepe has worked for more than three decades in girls' education, across the continent, and sees no difference geographically between students. But she observes that 14-year-olds now suffer more than their mothers or big sisters ever did, and many of the girls themselves acknowledge this. They attribute it to their own academic performance, or 'the curse of perfectionism'.

Kiepe is the first to raise with me the Little Miss Perfect syndrome, but over weeks and months of research it is raised again and again in Queensland, Victoria, New South Wales, South Australia and Tasmania by teachers and principals and school psychologists, all concerned about the debilitating effect it is having on some students. Flo Kearney, an experienced educator of young women, says that while some girls could deal with the Little Miss Perfect syndrome, others couldn't, and eating disorders and self-injury were sometimes the result. 'It's "I've got to be perfect", "I've got to achieve all this". It's quite sad,' she says. Kiepe says, 'They feel they have to have a balance between their school life and their extracurricular life, so they're trying to do everything they can and fit it all in,' she says. The impetus for this is partly driven by the wealth of opportunities on offer. Formal school lessons might begin and end at the school gate, but the ability to join Maths, Science or Coding clubs, participate in school dance, theatre or music ensembles, or represent a school in dozens of sports, means the school day beats the sun up on some mornings, and doesn't end until well into the night. Frequently a 14-year-old student will say to Kiepe, 'When I'm in Year 11 I'll have to really buckle down and get serious, but this is the lead-up so I'm trying to do as [many] extracurricular activities as I can.' 'But at the same time she's got the peer pressure and the parental pressure to gain high marks. She's competing with the friend who got the A in Maths and she's trying to get the A in Maths [herself],' Kiepe says.

In his book *The Triple Bind*, Dr Stephen Hinshaw paints a picture of teen girls, and the pressure they are under, that is generational; a bind their parents never found themselves in. 'The Triple Bind is possibly the greatest current threat to our daughters' health and well-being, an enormous obstacle to their becoming healthy, happy and successful adults,' he says. The triple bind refers to girls being good at all of the traditional girl activities, being good and competitive at traditional male activities, and conforming to 'a narrow, unrealistic set of standards that allows for no alternative'.[3] I remember his hypothesis being put at a parent–teacher night, when my daughters started at their new middle and high school. As the presenters were explaining Hinshaw's hypothesis I noticed parents around the room nodding. I ordered his book the next day. Contemporary girls, I learnt, needed to be pretty and sweet and nice. They needed to be athletic. Competitive. Academic, with offers into extension classes. They needed to be 'perfect'. School counsellors at my daughters' new school were warning new parents not to allow their children to take up every opportunity on offer. With many families coming from smaller schools, the lure of two dozen sports, academic clubs, arts, music and drama lessons, coding clubs and debating competitions had meant some 10- and 11-year olds were dead-tired and in tears by Friday. Leaving, I remember thinking that two activities a week would be a manageable number. And indeed that might work when you have two daughters. But what if you have more than two children, or there is a toddler in the house, or one of your children's talent stands out and they're required for more practice? The hours and days add up. A solid test of that is to try to make a weekday, after-school play date (oops, at 14 it's called 'hanging out', not a play date!) and you can see how scheduled our children's lives have become. Those good at netball might be required to train three days a week. The rowing champs don't win medals by getting up early once a month. To 'win' a position in the jazz band requires daily trumpet practice. The cello doesn't sound like the cello without designating 20 minutes a day to ironing out the musical bumps. Each debate eats up hours of preparation and practice. And all of that is on top of formal lessons, and the homework that schools believe is necessary to cement the daily learning.

For a moment, compare this to the schooling received by these 14-year-old girls' parents. Perhaps that will be your own schooling. I loved ballet, but gave it up to join speech and drama, and gave that up to join the debating team. I learnt tennis too, and chose it over other sports. If I wanted to enjoy running, or to practise sprinting, I was sent on laps around the block. Long jump might have been in the backyard. It wasn't scheduled, and the idea of adding to that list was not an option; both time, finances and the demands of five children provided a ceiling. So as the years progressed, I changed – from basketball to ballet, from swimming to speech and from drama to debating. It was a matter of choosing a passion; doing the lot of them was never an option. My friends were all the same. And while we didn't recognise it then, the downtime it provided us with stood us in good stead.

Brisbane Girls' Grammar School psychologist Jody Forbes tells students about the process involved in taking a photograph when she was their age. It's worth telling your own children, as I did, and watch their intrigue as you colour in the picture: how you prepared for the photograph before taking it. That's right, you were responsible for the focus. Then you waited until the other 11 or 23 photographs on the roll were taken. The expense of prints meant that that was never in the same day, or indeed the same week. Memories were built up over time. Once the roll was full, you'd take it down to the local pharmacy. That itself adds to the story. Dropping it off meant a trip on foot or in a car; downloading wasn't an option. A week later, you'd venture back to pick up the photographs with a delightful sense of anticipation. 'They don't understand delayed gratification,' Jody Forbes says. 'Now they just click and they've got it.' It's only an anecdote, but it points to the issue of persistence, and how it is now often lacking in our simple everyday transactions. Success, in the real world, comes from chipping away at things. A determination. Mastering something that is difficult can be boring and laborious in equal measure, but it is a good teacher. Not everything should come easily. In an instant, now, we can book a holiday online, buy a television, check a medical diagnosis and swap a sofa. Success is immediate. 'We send kids this idea that things are easy,' Jody says. 'Thomas Edison did not invent the light switch like that.' She clicks her fingers to make the point. 'That was thousands and thousands and thousands of failed experiments and people working together.' Boredom, and even disappointment, can feed the soul.

Dr Amanda Bell says a teen's capacity to deal with boredom has all but disappeared. Any free space and time is quickly filled with social media, apps and online interests. Bell sees a difference, often, between those teens brought up in country areas and their city cousins. Those on the land are more likely to have their spare time filled with real things, like helping feed animals or fixing the fence that's fallen down. Bell maintains that it is not nostalgia or melancholy or a glorifying of years past to recall that when most of our teen's parents – that's us – were growing up we'd be kicked out of the house after breakfast each weekend and told to go and amuse ourselves. 'And that was right up to when you were 15 or 16,' she says. That meant we were forced to consider the time ahead and to think, "Well alright, what am I going to do today?"' Headspace needed to be scheduled in as a priority, she says.

Before our 14-year-old daughters start rolling their eyes as they do when stories of 'in my time' surface, consider also the difference in expectations. Were you ever 'expected' to win the eisteddfod as well as the tennis match? Was there an expectation that an A+ showed you had done the required amount of study? No. Because the expectation placed on parents of adolescents was entirely different. You can almost hear Kim Kiepe shake her head, when asked about her time as a 14-year-old. 'I put myself back in the shoes of being a Year 9 student and I can remember vividly I wanted to be a high achiever,' she says. She remembers competing with her best friend in Maths, which wasn't her best subject, and neither of them wanting to reveal their mark to each other, just in case they were the one with the lower score. 'But that's as far as it went,' she says. 'I didn't feel the need to have to go and play volleyball and do my extracurricular ballet on a Saturday and be in the photography club and go and paint the orphanage in Fiji. All of those opportunities and experiences – I didn't have a fear I was missing out by not doing them. That's different to today.'

Each year, on an awards night, a prize is invariably given out to the all-rounder in a grade: the girl who stands tall against her peers across her studies, her sport and her performing arts. When Kiepe was a teacher in the 1980s, she remembers the all-rounders standing out. They were natural; blessed with an ability. There was only ever one or two, never more. That was still the case as much as 20 years later, when she was at St Hilda's School on Queensland's Gold Coast. Then, Kiepe was involved in choosing the all-rounder. Perhaps there were three contenders. It was always difficult, but it was one of three who would be chosen. Now, she says, there can be 'two handfuls' of equally qualified girls. 'And it's very hard to say who is the best all-rounder,' she says.

All of this has another consequence. What about those girls who aren't in extension class, or fighting for As? What about the beautiful souls who will talk to the person isolated at lunchtime but does not have a hope in Hades of making the netball team or the coding club? These girls might still go to university, and are equally likely to change their part of the world. Despite that, do they sit on the sidelines here? Do they miss out? 'I do wonder about those girls in the middle and I worry about them being the lost girls,' Kiepe says. With honour boards boasting the same girls' names time and time again, and with the student chosen for the exchange program being the one whose name is registered under 'prefects', Kiepe is concerned. 'Schools have to do a better job of making sure those lost girls – those girls in the middle – are not disregarded; that they have their moments to shine.'

A silver lining exists here, and it's important for 14-year-old girls – and their parents – to know this. 'I think those sorts of girls are those who go on to have university lives that are relatively bump-free,' Kiepe says. Her rationale, supported by many others, is this: if school is a journey along a road littered with potholes, and some girls have been tripped up by their fair share, they've developed resilience. That's why, perhaps, so many high achievers accepted into their first choice of university course end up dropping out. Kiepe says she's a living example of the 'relatively middle-of-the-road achiever who wasn't sporty'. 'I went on to have a relatively smooth journey compared to those girls who've experienced eating disorders and those things that manifest with anxiety.' Dr Bell sees high achievers arrive daily on the doorstep of The Women's College at Sydney University. 'We see some great kids come in here who have been school captain, they've done this, they've done that, they've been on exchange, they've been to Chile. Then they come to university and they're dog-tired. They just can't do it anymore,' she says.

The problem here, perhaps, is our lack of truthfulness with our own children. How many fathers tell their daughters they didn't do the top Maths subject? Or gild the lily on their Biology marks? At the other end, students sitting in a Year 9 class being taught Biology will expect their teacher to have topped their class in science. Kiepe says Maths was not her biggest strength and she struggled with it. 'How ironic that I became an accounting teacher! I refer to that in my interview with the new girls.' She says she remembers her fear and anxiety in Maths class. She felt like 'a rabbit in the headlights, frozen at the table' if she was asked to calculate a complex ratio. It was only later that accounting became a passion.

Role models play an important part here, too. Repeatedly, principals say that 'the girls will be it once they see it'. That's why staff often choose former students over visiting 'celebrities' to talk at awards nights and other ceremonies, for it permits students to make the link between homegrown and success. 'Success after school is about so many things, and that's something we really really try to talk to our girls about,' says Jane Danvers. She says her experience has shown that most of those role models had arrived at success through the mistakes they'd made along the way. 'We need to be far more open about those journeys,' she says.

An irony sits behind the education system, as it stands now. So much emphasis is put on filling the academic bucket. Study. Extra classes. Extension. Tuition. NAPLAN. External tests. Online learning, to creep past a classmate. League tables to show the most successful schools. And we celebrate that. A good report card can be a trip to the movies. $30 for each A. But those in charge of the system are warning constantly that it is becoming too academically focused. School no longer finishes at Year

12. It factors in what university course a student is aiming for. And which town or city that university is located in becomes the measure of success. 'I think that particularly young women do put a lot of pressure on themselves to succeed academically and that negative perfectionism is something that we are really dealing with,' Danvers says. And that can translate into a situation where a 14-year-old wants to do so well that she freezes and is unable to take the next step.

Judith Tudball, principal of St. Mary's Anglican School in WA, says students need to understand that employers are looking for more than good marks, and that girls need to broaden their horizons. 'They are not just looking for a top academic score; they are looking for the students who volunteered, who've given time to service, who've travelled, who have team leadership skills, who have critical thinking skills on the spot,' she says. Tudball likes the shift, where broader skills are given greater value. 'The score is important, but if we can be developing a school of girls who have a broad outlook on life and who take the focus in this narcissistic world away from themselves and think of others and give to others, then we're headed in the right direction.'

We are on the brink of a related change here too, perhaps. The current areas of growth are around innovation and creativity. A kaleidoscope of new fields is opening up, and the pathway to success does not always pass through university. 'What we need to do is give them the underlying skills to make those choices and navigate them,' Danvers says. Principal of Santa Sabina College in Strathfield, Sydney, Dr Maree Herrett agrees. She says that the changing employment landscape can also add to the anxiety felt amongst 14- and 15-year-old girls. She says a recent chat with Year 10 students illustrated the point. They were anxious about achieving. She kept asking questions, digging deeper. 'They're worried because they live in Sydney and it's so expensive,' she says. They're worried about whether they will ever even have the opportunity to leave home. 'There's an uncertainty about it. Young people are growing up into an employment market that will largely be casualised and contract-driven. It's sold to them as fabulous,' she says. While they are told that they'll have several different careers over their work life, that brings with it enormous uncertainty. 'Will they ever be able to afford to go to university? Will they ever be able to buy a house? They are the messages that are, in part, driving the anxiety: that it is going to be tough out there,' Herrett says.

Isobel has been taking anxiety medication for 12 months, just after she had a falling out with friends. She doesn't understand the medication's fine print, but her parents believe it will settle the nerves that had her refusing to leave the car at drop-off time. She's not embarrassed by the medication, she says, because some of her friends take it too. They didn't talk about it, she says, because it was no big deal. This, perhaps, is one of the many hidden pointers to the epidemic of anxiety sweeping high schools. 'The majority of girls are highly strung,' one school nurse says. 'I have to get them to chill out,' a school counsellor says. 'I say to them, "Stop studying. I need you to fail. I want you to bomb out on this physics test. I need you to dip your toe in and know what failure is like, because if you go through school and you succeed at everything you do and have never had to deal with disappointment or failure, you're going to be in fear of that and avoiding failure for your whole life". We know that those girls crash and burn.' It's a big ask for a 14-year-old who is within striking distance of being a subject dux or captaining the class debate team and whose parents proudly tell everyone that she's on-course to become an architect.

Boys. Boys. Boys

*'There's pressure to do things and then
they tell everyone. And then other
people think you're a bad person.'*

ELIZA,
14

Taylor Swift is belting out 'Bad Blood', as the young teens take over the basketball stadium, currently being used as the school dance floor.

At this all-girls' school, Taylor Swift will go on to be a favourite, sharing the strobe lights with Katie Perry and Justin Bieber. Up next, Swift tells the crowd it's time to 'Shake It Off'.

The local boys' schools have been invited to attend tonight, and hundreds pour through the door. Security is tight. These children are just into their teens, 13 and 14, and the school knows anything that can go wrong can affect its reputation for years. Teachers patrol upstairs, looking down onto the dance floor. Outside, security personnel pace back and forth. Volunteers man the drinking fountain, the exits and the cloakroom.

The dress code is strict. Closed-in shoes only. No short shorts. Shoulders must be covered. The girls abide by these rules. Many of them met earlier, to dress together, amidst a sea of giggles and laughs. It's delightful for the girls, and for their parents. They drop them off with a promise to be back for pick-up at 9.30 pm. Once inside, no student is allowed to leave until that time. Inside the cloakroom, the winter coats come off. Some of the girls have dressed as tradies, others as cheerleaders. Some arrive in flowery sundresses meant for another season. Others are in short skirts they hitch up to make a touch shorter. Others, once inside, quickly pull their tops off the shoulder. 'It's the look, don't you know?'

Inside, volunteer parents are briefed. Photographs of others, and selfies, are not allowed. Neither are amorous embraces. Outstretched arms, on each other's shoulders, is as close as it should get tonight. The boys look so much bigger. An average 14-year-old boy is 4 cm taller than a 14-year-old girl, and 4 kilograms heavier. Tonight, many of them dwarf the girls as they wait to be asked to dance. Most of the girls are huddled together – there's strength in numbers – but after a few dances, they get the hang of it. 'Seven times,' one tells her friends. Translated, seven different boys have asked for her phone number. 'I wasn't quite so lucky. I only got four,' one says in the car on the way home. To them, it's a game. Their expectations are not that anyone will call – indeed, one of them didn't know her own number and provided her suitors with her father's number – but they are chuffed to have been asked. Deep inside the dance floor, at least one volunteer is hard at work breaking up young couples. Some girls are not so keen on the number of suitors they rack up but on one suitor in particular. Arms on each other's shoulders, they take every opportunity to quickly slide their head onto their dance partner's shoulder. With 1000 children, volunteers are outnumbered and relationships are born. Later, one tells her friend about the cute boy who asked her to go out with him. He's tall. He's good looking. He rows. She already feels so close to him. He's the whole package. 'What's his name?' her friend asks. Andrew, she thinks. She's not quite sure.

At the school tuckshop the next day, the talk amongst the mothers turns to the outfits the girls wore. At a nearby boys' school, one mother says, volunteers hand out fluorescent vests for those girls wearing inappropriate attire. A debate breaks out. Is that shaming the young women? Or protecting them? Another mum has worked in the cloakroom at another boys' school. She tells of how girls are often dropped off wearing a dress and then slip into the restrooms, remove it, and take to the dance floor in flimsy shorts and tops, styled on a bra. 'I swear you need to check what they are wearing *under* the dress, from my experience,' she says. It goes without saying that they pull the dress back on before being picked up by their parents.

The three-hour dance is instructive in the dilemma 14-year-old girls face. Of course boys face the same type of issues. Will she dance with me? Am I confident enough to ask her to dance? What happens if she says 'no'? Do I ask for her phone number? But for girls, the issues are full of irony. Next week they might be working late to ensure they steal a debate from under the local boys' school's noses. Yet on this night they wouldn't dream of approaching a boy; they will wait patiently, with fingers crossed, to be asked to dance by the 'right' boy. In Maths, the next day, they will be as competitive as hell, trying to out-class the lad sitting at the next desk. But tonight, many of them will encourage the same boys with their already-short skirt hitched a touch higher. They count the night's success in the number of teenage boys who want their phone number, or whether by the time the lights come up on this high school dance they're 'someone special' to someone else. They change their behaviour, play down the wit and the smarts they have in the classroom. Being competitive with the boys in the class is a given. But it comes with a rider – as long as they can still 'catch' (their word, repeatedly) a boy.

Despite the enormous effort made by educators, girls don't get a lot of help to solve the quandary they find themselves in. Just look at the advice they receive. Teen magazines are all about how they can transform their crush into their boyfriend. Or how best to make a boy like them. The kudos of arriving at school on Monday dating a boy is colossal. And then, parenting experts say, some mums add to the problem by announcing to all and sundry the next morning on Facebook that their gorgeous girl is quite taken with this 'perfect lad'.

My aim with this book was to find out the challenges 14-year-old girls face – from their perspective. And it was clear that 'boys' featured highly. In one focus group of 30 14-year-olds, I asked them what topic they most wanted advice on. 'Boys.' 'Boys.' 'Boys.' It was the same answer, over and over again, at public schools and private schools. 'I want to know about having a crush on a boy and you really want to tell him but he feels differently to you,' says Sophie. 'What about when they lead you on for ages and then just ditch you?' asks Courtney. 'Why do they lead you on?' asks Hannah. Lucy says she's 'not interested in them. Boys only like stunning girls' – before explaining it was important to 'get one'. Olivia does not live in the same state as Lucy but her answer is almost identical. 'Boys just want a girl who is stunning. If you are not, then they're just not into you,' she says. Olivia admitted to finding that hard, because she believed that no-one would find her stunning.

For all the education our daughters have received on equality and positive self-image, that made me feel – as a mother – that we are on the brink of failing our gorgeous girls. Good looks equal success – at least in their eyes. Pretty equals popular. Stunners deserve a boyfriend. The wallflowers deserve to miss out. Crucially, it's not that they think boys just *want* attractive, sassy girls; this seems to be their verdict on who *deserves* a boyfriend. Educator and author Dannielle Miller says girls sometimes make the mistake of thinking that looks will bring them love. That's why, she says, they seek 'likes' on their social media accounts, for example. She says in *Loveability*: 'But you know what? Girls who don't fit conventional notions of beauty and girls who do are equally likely to have successful relationships. We mustn't fall into the trap of trying to measure our loveability via the mirror or a set of scales.'[1]

So how many 14-year-olds believe they are currently in a relationship? The answers here are bewildering. 'I think I'm in one,' one says. 'If all goes well,' another adds. 'I'm just waiting to hear,' a third says. 'Getting there, but I don't know if he likes me back.' 'No, not yet, but I'm trying.' 'I wish.' Those more certain of their relationships were not particularly at ease, however. Kerrie says, 'I have a boyfriend but my parents don't know.' And Rosalie

says, '[My biggest worry is] getting caught sneaking out
to meet my boyfriend.' Jessica didn't tell her parents this,
either: 'I was talking to someone [whom she wanted to
date] and he turned out to be much older than he said
to me. It was awful.' And Monica: 'My biggest worry is
my boyfriend dumping me.' Where, one wonders, is that
boldness seen in class?

This story is a run-of-the-mill one. Last year, Tia got a
boyfriend. For Tia's mother – and her boyfriend's mother
– it was tough; a wild ride of constant texts, trying to
get Tia back to her desk to do homework, and then tears
when it ended. 'It was crazy and distracting . . . hundreds
of texts a day, and I mean hundreds . . . Eventually I rang
the boy's mother – who I knew – and said, "We need to
have an agreement. We need to agree that there is no
texting after 9 pm."' The boy's mother acquiesced. Tia's
mother was disturbed by how her bright, bold daughter
received validation from the attention she got – not just
from the boy, but from her girlfriends. 'It delivered such
social acceptance,' she says. 'When they first got together
– and I think all they did was text – she jumped notches
with her girlfriends. All of a sudden, she was popular. She
was even invited to more parties.' But it turned topsy-turvy
when the break-up happened, only a few weeks later. 'Her
friends dropped her. Her boyfriend equalled social kudos,
and that's really sad . . . As a mother, I don't know how

you get them to see they've got their whole life in front of them. She genuinely couldn't see past the next text.'

Take the texts out of the equation and perhaps that scenario is not too different from our own Year 9 experiences. Doodling the name of our love-interest on our pad. Staring out the window wondering when the next time might be that we would meet. And, if we got so lucky as to actually have our crush reciprocated, feeling the heartbreak when it all (inevitably) came to an end. But while contemporary romances can mirror our own at that age, a different issue arises, often, when a relationship now sours. Tia's mother is grateful her daughter escaped that. 'We talked about sex and she [made] the point that those who partake are rarely still with that boy a month later – and then she has a name. I said to her, "Do you want that name, or not?"' That's not new, either – a point made by Peggy Orenstein in her book *Girls & Sex*. She says that 'despite the seismic changes in expectations and opportunity', girls were still subject to double standards where she was termed a 'slut' for being sexually active, while her male peer was a 'player'. 'Now, though, girls who abstain from sex, once thought of as the "good girls", are shamed as well, labelled "virgins" or "prudes". As one high school senior said to me, "usually the opposite of a negative is a positive, but in this case it's two negatives". So what are they supposed to do?'[2]

It seems girls are on a hiding to nothing. At a packed Business Chicks breakfast in Brisbane in 2016, domestic violence campaigner Rosie Batty told the audience that she remembers, as a 14-year-old, how you were catalogued as either a 'slut or untouchable'. The best question came from a 17-year-old girl. Many of her friends had started having boyfriends, but some of the boys talked badly about the girls to their friends. How should they deal with that?

The answer is not simple. I was sitting next to Kylie Lang, a popular newspaper columnist in Brisbane who had previously lashed out in newsprint over the slut-shaming of young women. 'A 14-year-old girl is recorded having sex with boys her age at a party,' Lang wrote. 'One boy posts the video online and a friend of the girl shares it. What happens next? The girl who had sex is "slut-shamed" at school by her peers while the boys, on a campus not too far away, are a source of amusement to their cohort.'[3] Lang is spot-on here. 'Why are girls held to a different standard than boys? Who sets these standards and why should we accept them?'

Last year, the revelation that 70 schools were being targeted in a pornography ring where teen boys were secretly swapping graphic sexual images of their female peers made headlines and prompted a police investigation. The poses of many of the girls were shocking, but perhaps more shocking was the language the teenage boys used to describe their peers. In another episode, students at a private boys' school set up a 'young sluts' Instagram account for the purpose of voting on the 'slut of the year'. On every measure, both those episodes were vile, immature and disgusting – and made headlines. But the girls tell of other incidents too, where they become the unsuspecting targets of campaigns to exploit and shame them. These include cases of ex-boyfriends setting up fake accounts to ridicule them or new boyfriends who secretly record their dalliances and forward it on to others. They're on a smaller scale, so they've avoided the headlines.

But why do our 14-year-olds, in a world where they will blog on the subject of equality or do a 5000-word presentation on third-world women, not rise up against such episodes? Why is it that the above episodes are only revealed as a result of parents stumbling upon an account, or a journalist running a commentary piece, or a school acting on a complaint? 'Many girls have boyfriends and then they [the boys] pressure other girls to kiss boys and do other things,' Beth explains. 'Most boys want more than one girl. And I learnt the hard way,' Alice says. Beth and Alice are 14.

So let's take a step back. A relationship, at the age of 14, might involve incessant texting. It might mean a milkshake in the mall on a Friday afternoon, enveloped by a big group of other teenagers. It might even mean a movie on a Thursday night, unchaperoned. But how do you know if your daughter is having sex? And what does 'sex' even mean to a 14-year-old girl?

Two major national surveys capture those results. The Australian Study of Health and Relationships (ASHR) is conducted every decade, and in 2013 it included 20 094 men and women aged 16–69. They were chosen using random-digit dialling of landline and mobile phones. One of its findings was that the median age of first intercourse was 17 and that about 50 per cent of people had had intercourse for the first time when aged 16, 17 or 18.[4] The second survey – the 2014 National Survey of Australian Secondary Students and Sexual Health[5] – involved more than 2000 students in Years 10, 11 and 12 at government, Catholic and independent schools in all states and territories. It showed that 25 per cent of Year 10 students, 33 per cent of Year 11s and 50 per cent of Year 12s reported having had sex. Just under one-quarter – 23 per cent – of sexually active students had had sex with three or more people in the past year, while an astonishing 25 per cent of sexually active students reported an experience of unwanted sex of some kind. More reassuringly, 50 per cent of those who had not had intercourse felt good about this decision. (That was driven more by personal decision-making, according to the survey, than religion, culture or pressure from parents.)

Those figures relate to intercourse, but as Dr Melissa Kang, GP for *Dolly* magazine for the past 23 years, says, most girls have had 'some form of sexual experience by the end of Year 12'. 'At 14, the majority certainly have not had vaginal intercourse but a significant – or even a majority – have had some intimate feelings with somebody else.' Kang says this involves physical contact of a sexual nature – like kissing and light petting. She adds that puberty catapults all adolescents into a new body and a whole new set of sensations. She says most of the advice sought by 14-year-olds is around the anxiety and confusion that comes with those involuntary feelings of arousal. And the most common question asked? 'There's a real anxiety around whether their bodies are normal,' says Dr Kang. 'One thing I've noticed in the past ten years, which was not prevalent before, is an anxiety about genital appearance.' That, most experts agree, is sheeted home to the impact of pornography and the modern trend of removing pubic hair.

Kang is eager to point out that the 14-year-old's interest in boys is perfectly normal and natural. Rebecca Sparrow, in her fabulous book *Ask Me Anything*, addresses anonymous questions from teen girls. It highlights that interest.

'I'm ugly. So how will I ever get a boyfriend?'

'Is it normal to be 14 and NOT know any guys?'

'What do you do when all your friends have boyfriends and you don't?'

'How do you know if a boy likes you?'

'How do you say NO to guys.'

That last question begs for an answer that every parent wants her daughter to know. Teenage expert Michelle Mitchell says being 14 can be a crucial time for decision-making. 'They are at quite high risk of making a decision around sex that is probably relatively uneducated and naive, and I think it is something that parents have to have their eyes open to,' she says. Mitchell tells her high school sexual health classes about a teen and the Facebook message she sent to her boyfriend who was wanting her to have sex. 'I don't get why your virginity is so important to you!!! Its not like it's a treasure chest or anything!!!!' he wrote. This is what she retorted with: 'Well it is like a treasure chest to me. And let's just say that your key is definitely not big enough to unlock it.' Mitchell says teenagers need 'cool comeback lines' which help them say 'NO' when they feel pressured to go further than they would like. On her michellemitchell.org blog, she gives a ready-reckoner of lines, like these:

Pressure Line: We have been together for a long time, why don't you want to do it?

Comeback Line: Because I'm not ready. If you are waiting around until I am you may be waiting a long time.

Pressure Line: Everyone else is doing it.

Comeback Line: I'm not everyone.

Pressure Line: I won't tell anyone.

Comeback Line: Everyone tells someone.

Parenting expert Maggie Dent says that, increasingly, girls at 14 want to have a boyfriend – but what 'have a boyfriend' means covers a wide spectrum. She says it's crucial, at this time, for girls to have a support network of genuine girlfriends. A lifetime of work has shown her that, if enveloped in a big group of girlfriends, our 14-year-olds are less likely to take risks or 'hunt for belonging in all the wrong places'. It helps them keep their self-identity, outside any relationship.

One consequence of that, you would think, is that the heartbreak might be less. When Dent's view is explained, a school nurse nods. With decades of experience, she says she gets sad seeing where girls go looking for love and acceptance. 'They crave physical contact and they go and look for it. There's that pressure to have a boyfriend. Girls pressure other girls. They are such babies in Years 7 and 8, and Year 9 is where they see themselves as bigger and they are looking for that physical connection. That's part of their sexual growth – but often it's looking for love in all the wrong places. They think they're special to someone. Someone really really likes me. So when [the boys] don't like them, or they decide they like someone better, it is diabolical.'

The acknowledgement of transgender students is also now making inroads into schools and the issue will only grow, further making it difficult for some 14-year-olds to find the sense of belonging they yearn. 'Everyone wants to fit in somewhere,' one teacher explains. She says that our children are taught to speak up, and they were now brave enough to do that. She says, increasingly, a student will openly say they are gay, bisexual or transgender. Some schools were well-equipped to deal with those conversations; others were not.

While that heartache over young love and sexual identity is not exclusive to this generation, *Dolly* doctor Melissa Kang says many parents have learnt from their own parents. 'Parents have a lot of trouble talking about sex, or it's talked about in terms of "make sure you use protection" or "you're too young to be having sex".' It was important, she says, for parents to ensure they did not just provide their children with a narrow message about the dangers of sex, because their child was not thinking about contraception or sexually transmissible infections. 'They're really thinking about "Well am I attractive, can I kiss properly?" – that's a common question I get: "Am I doing this right?"' Parents need to do a much better job of being the primary sex educators from a young age and stop thinking that talking to your child about sex is going to make them go and have sex, because all the evidence points against that. Having good communication, giving your child access to the resources they might need and respecting that they might need to do that in private – at least initially – is really important.' Kang says telling a 14-year-old that sex was something they shouldn't be asking about meant they were unlikely to front up and ask again at 16, when they were planning to have sex. 'I encourage parents to take the view that, "Well I think you're too young now but perhaps sometime in the next couple of years you might feel as though you are ready, and I'd like you to be able to come and talk to me about it, but if you're not then I think we'll help you find a GP you can trust" – that sort of thing – or "Here are some good websites you can go to", or "Is there someone in the extended family you could go to?". If the average is 16, 16 and a half, it's no use waiting until then to have this conversation. It's better to be prepared.'

That's the case for another reason, too – one that really only seems to be the domain of nasty news headlines, but one that police are increasingly seeing. Jon Rouse, the head of Task Force Argos, says parents are kidding themselves if they believe their 14-year-old hasn't seen pornography. Freely accessible websites are being shared by 14-year-old boys – and that's where many of them are learning points on sex. Indeed, porn was becoming the dominant 'sex educator', two teen experts told me. 'Boys are looking at this and it is where they are learning what is "normal",' one said. Senior Constable Kelly Humphries says it is not unusual to find a teen who genuinely does not understand the concept of consent. 'They don't know what it means. Yes or No. Was it a Yes? I don't really know. Was permission given? I don't really know. So it's all about where they get their information from,' she says. Pornography was confusing decision-making, too. 'They think that love is choking, that she wants to be held around the neck. Or you give her a slap first.' Why? Because that is what they see on the internet. 'I know that's not most 14-year-olds,' Humphries says. 'But some 14-year-olds we are dealing with are exposed to that.'

Former police officer and author Susan McLean says another issue has begun to concern her, and that is the willingness of girls to 'put up with stuff without telling anyone'. From her experience, they had a 'tolerance level', particularly for online abuse. 'I often get asked, "How much abuse should I tolerate before I tell someone?" I don't know where that's coming from but it's so wrong, because I can see if a girl will tolerate online abuse she's more likely to tolerate sexual abuse and physical abuse and psychological abuse because she believes there is a certain level [of acceptability],' she says.

One final pointer here, because it is so important to those who are at the centre of this book: privacy. It's a message that the girls delivered over and over again. Where once they didn't mind their little brother scampering into their room when they were 11 or 12, they don't want it now. They want to lie on their bed, in their own dreamy world. They want to listen to music, sometimes even dance with no-one watching. 'That's absolutely classic, normal development, particularly in the years of puberty,' Kang says. It's not only privacy they're seeking, it's solitude. It comes with that day-dreamy behaviour that kicks in at puberty. 'I think some of that is self-consciousness about their bodies, but some of it is actually what is going on in their brains.' Kang says it is really important for parents to respect that and to give their adolescents more space, but at the same time it's important to maintain connection. She's not talking here about the door being physically shut, or open – that's an individual thing. Her point is that parents should fight the urge to back off; they needed to focus on walking a tightrope between being too nosey and being uninterested. 'My advice to parents is to find the balance but do not disconnect,' Kang says. And that's probably particularly the case when it comes to teen parties . . .

It's my party . . .

'My daughter was up-front; she asked me at
what age I first kissed a boy. I was a bit taken
aback, because if I was honest, it was 14!'

MICHELLE,
mother of a 14-year-old

At Sarah's 14th birthday party, the invitees quickly split. The girls from her dance class latched onto the karaoke machine and started belting out tunes, taking turns to dance under the strobe lights like no-one was watching. Sarah's mother was keeping an eye on things, and could hear them loudly from the kitchen where she was putting pizza onto plates. At 9 pm she dropped down and observed the second group. They were from Sarah's high school – delightful girls she had met many times. She knew most of their parents, too, from netball and choir in middle school. But this cohort was not interested in singing out loud tonight. As Sarah laid out the pizza, this group didn't look up. They were huddled in a corner, around her 15-year-old nephew, playing a game of truth and dare. She listened, as best she could, and it sounded innocent enough, but she went back upstairs intrigued by the completely different interests of two groups of friends. Her younger daughter, an expert in eavesdropping (as so many siblings are), told her the next morning that they were talking about sex. But the party soon took on a more innocent character. 'Eventually the school kids left and the dancing girls stayed overnight. They could have watched anything under the sun – and they picked *High School Musical*. They joked about it, saying it was really funny. They were watching it from the perspective of a 14-year-old,' Sarah's mother says.

At another party, this one celebrating Erin's 14th birthday, everything is different from the time it kicks off at 6 pm. The music is louder. The lights are lower. No-one's singing, or dancing. The boys and girls huddle in groups, but some of them – especially the boys – seem much older than 14. Two of them were stopped from bringing alcohol into Erin's home, earlier in the evening. One principal I spoke to explains what might happen next. 'There's also a lot of that hyper-sexualised behaviour with parties which parents may or may not know about where there's all the inappropriate behaviour between the genders – casual sex, frequently with multiple part-ners at that age – most definitely,' she says. This is the principal of a big girls' school. 'Drinking. Drugs clearly. But drinking is bigger at the moment. And drinking and sexual behaviour and rape go hand and hand. And the girls are not necessarily calling the rape [for what it is], for all the reasons a lot of people don't call rape.' Another girls' school principal says parents are unaware of some of the practices happening at some of these parties. 'We are teaching girls here about respecting themselves and standing up for themselves. And then what they let themselves get involved in, it really saddens me and it deeply disturbs me. We really try to protect them from themselves.' She says boys' schools are putting focused effort into teaching them how to treat women. 'We know they are teaching them, but then I have to deal with what happens after the parties … it just appals me.'

The two parties for Sarah and Erin show the almighty chasm that plays out in holding 14-year-old birthday parties. It's a ramshackle continuum, as one teacher put it to me, that travels from treasure hunts to high teas, from dressing up and going on shopping ventures to having a make-up artist provide group lessons, through to disco parties, private parties and out-of-control celebrations that can ruin reputations, and lives.

The girls – 14-year-olds – sit on the brink, even admit-ting that they want to score an invitation to the 'adult'-type functions, but often breathing a sigh of relief when they don't. 'People our age are pressured into doing a lot of stuff like drinking and boys, but as soon as you say no you get shamed for not doing it,' Meaghan says. 'Then if you do something you get called names that are rude and people just don't think before they speak to you.' Elizabeth says that she feels pressured to 'do things' that her mother might have confronted at the age of 16, not 14. 'There's a lot more pressure to do some things, like drink and drugs and sex,' she says. That means, often, parents are not told how a party might unfold. 'It's a hard situation when your parents don't understand what is expected of you at our age. There have been many situations where I don't tell my parents that there is going to be drinking at a party and they find out about it, but not from me. and I get in a lot of trouble,' says Harriet. And Yvette: 'Next year it will become the norm, but a lot of people are doing it already.'

But what is the norm? And is there such a thing? And how do you know if your daughter, when you're not watching, is dancing and singing like a 12-year-old, or tempted to wander off into the bush, a bottle of vodka in hand and sex on her mind?

'I always say for girls it's 14 and for boys it's 15 – when everything starts to change and parenting becomes a real challenge,' Paul Dillon says. Dillon is the director of Drug and Alcohol Research and Training Australia (DARTA) and has been working in the area of drug education for more than 25 years. He bears good news. 'What we do know about school-based 14-year-old girls is that they have some of the lowest rates of illicit drug use since records began.' That's a big tick, particularly since records go back two decades. And it runs counter to the popular media perception that this generation of teens is out of control. Cannabis use, for example, is at half the level it was in 1996. Even tobacco smoking is now old hat, and it's increasingly rare to see a 14-year-old light up at the back of a bus stop. Those points should be celebrated. Often, it's easy to pick on the young, but smoking is a really good example of how public education has influenced this generation. Ask a 40-something friend. We all tried it. Some of us got addicted and spent years trying to kick the habit. Our children turn their noses up at that now. 'Mum, I can't believe you would have been so stupid. Why did you even have one in the first place?' my kids say. Another friend, who still has the odd cigarette, admits to waiting until the children go to bed before sneaking out onto the back balcony to get her nicotine hit. When questioned, she's not worried about being a bad example, or the health consequences of her habit. She's worried her teens 'will catch her'. How times change!

The statistics make that real. The Australian Secondary Students' Alcohol and Drug survey began in 1984. In 2014, 23 000 secondary students aged between 12 and

17 years participated in the survey and were asked about their use of tobacco, alcohol, analgesics, tranquilisers and illicit substances. So let's take smoking. In 2014, 94 per cent of 12-year-olds had no experience with smoking, which decreased to 61 per cent among 17-year-olds. Only 3 per cent of all students had smoked more than 100 cigarettes in their lifetime, and only 5 per cent of all 12- to 17-year-old students were current smokers. 'The proportions of 12- to 15-year-old students who had smoked in their lifetime, in the past month and in the past week in 2014 were significantly lower than the proportions found in 2011 and 2008 and were the lowest since the survey series began,' the report stated.[1]

Alcohol consumption follows a similar trajectory. Just under 25 000 secondary students aged between 12 and 17 years participated in this survey in 2011. 'The proportion of 12- to 15-year-olds drinking in the seven days before the survey decreased significantly between 2005 (22 per cent) and 2011 (11 per cent) and between 2008 (17 per cent) and 2011,' it said. The percentage of 14-year-old girls who recorded drinking in the past seven days was 10.7 per cent. Forty-four per cent of the same age group said they had used alcohol in the last year, and 20.5 per cent of 14-year-old girls said they had drunk alcohol in the previous month. 'Among 12- to 15-year-olds, the prevalence of current drinking declined during the 1980s, then increased in the 1990s, peaking in 2002. Among

12- to 15-year-olds, the prevalence of current drinking began to decrease after 2002 and this decrease has continued into 2011,' said the report.[2] But despite this good news, it is still alcohol that will snag many of our youngsters. 'This is certainly the drug that most parents are going to have a problem with with their kids, and certainly for girls we see alcohol start a little earlier than young men,' Paul Dillon says.

Associate Professor James Scott is from the University of Queensland Centre for Clinical Research. A child and adolescent psychiatrist, he offers two ways to explain the effect of drugs and alcohol on the 14-year-old brain. In the first case, part of the brain wants to go out and have a good time, while another part is charged with putting the brakes on and warning that it is not a good idea. 'When we drink alcohol or take drugs, that removes some of the effects of the frontal part of the brain,' Scott says. This is the part that governs our reasoning. 'That happens to all of us,' Scott continues. 'Take an adolescent. The front part of the brain is not that mature anyway, then you add alcohol or drugs and it really doesn't work. They can get themselves into all sorts of trouble.' The second effect of some drugs is to overload the brain, change neural pathways, damage cells and lead to a greater dependence on the drug. But while early-onset drinking and cannabis use might lead to addiction, Scott says for many young people it was the act of taking the drugs that led to problems. 'Adolescents are already a bit uninhibited ... and then they make really bad decisions,' he says. Other experts also warn that the immediate effect of alcohol – feeling tipsy – fed the immediate gratification that this generation relies on; and impulsiveness could lead to a lifetime of regret.

Paul Dillon says that, realistically, illicit drugs are not part of a 14-year-old girl's world – and most might not even have had any exposure to them. But there are two riders to this good news about a drop in use, for while drug use has fallen across the board, two groups continue to dominate in a teen's use of drugs. The first is the 14-year-old cohort who have left the school gates by that age. They will make the headlines about 14-year-old drug users. The second is a group more likely to mix with, and even influence, your 14-year-old, and that is the group comprising the socially and often physically mature teen girls who are friendly with older boys. Dillon says, 'It's a very small group but it's a group that is very obvious and very influential. They are usually the girls who mature physically earlier. They're usually the pretty girls; they're the girls that all the other girls want to be like and they're the girls the boys want to go out with.'

This is the group commonly called the TCs, short for the Too Cools. It doesn't mean every girl who signs up to be a TC is out drinking, but from Dillon's experience that's usually where the drinkers are drawn from. 'I think a lot of us who work in the parenting area call them the evil princesses,' he says. 'They really are a [powerful] group of girls ... and often not particularly very nice people, but they have a lot of influence. Also, because they are so obvious, they often warp everyone's perception of what is going on amongst that age group.'

Dillon says he regularly argues with schools where principals tell him they are worried about the drinking culture that has enveloped the Year 9 cohort. 'I say, you do not have all of your 14-year-olds drinking. You have a very small group and you know who they are. Everyone knows who they are.' Almost without exception, he says, they'll be the girls who are hanging out with 16-year-old boys. 'Usually, you hear them speaking about cannabis at parties ... their boyfriends are smoking, those kinds of things.' Dillon doesn't wrap his views in any sort of political correctness. When a teen turns 15, often their parents 'become total morons' and allow them to go to dance festivals and other such events where adult supervision is minimal, he says. 'What we know at 14 is that they really are in the midst of adolescence, and starting to mature and trying to find their place in the world.'

A security guard at a conference I was emceeing starts talking about how he could write a book about 14-year-old girls. He works at a nightclub in Brisbane's Fortitude Valley. He says he routinely picks up a 14-year-old pretending to be 18. Two years ago, he says, these girls would have a fake licence that looked like a fake licence. Then they got more professional; they looked like any other licence or university ID card. That's when he and his colleagues decided to start asking teens to show them their Facebook accounts. They all carried a phone, so it was an easy matter to ask them to pull it out and show him. Invariably it would prove them to be years younger than 18. But this group was clever, he said. They now had fake Facebook accounts, all with their ages registered as 18. How does he know they are not genuinely 18? 'You just do, love,' he says. 'I've been doing this for a long time.' He suggests parents search their child's name on Facebook or other social media sites – and they might find they have two: same photograph, same content, but different registered ages.

Ask a school nurse and they'll tell you of dozens of overheard conversations in which 14-year-olds openly boast of their alcohol and drug use. One says, from her recent experience, 'pot has crept into use too'. The most vulnerable individuals, from her experience, are the quiet ones, sometimes the quirky ones, or those who haven't quite found their own tribe. Sometimes those in separated or combined families, with older step-siblings, have easy access to illicit substances – and travelling between parents can make it difficult to police. 'Everyone seems to have a boyfriend now,' this school nurse says. 'It's the thing to do, because of pressure.' She agrees with Dillon: it's the 14-year-old cohort, with older boyfriends, who talk constantly about parties and 'how funny' such and such was while 'smashed'.

In speaking to experts, the role of parents tops the pops again, and mothers butting up against their daughters, and vice versa, plays a big role here. All of a sudden their little girls, who enjoyed girlie things with their mums, are looking sideways at 16- and 17-year-old boys. Sometimes they'll come home and reveal that they're a teeny-weeny bit interested in someone. 'My daughter was up-front; she asked me at what age I first kissed a boy. I was a bit taken aback, because if I was honest, it was 14!' says Michelle. 'She told me her pulse started to race every time she saw this bloke. I took a deep breath and said that was perfectly normal.' Other girls will not whisper a word about their feelings or activities, some believing they'd be in trouble with their parents. But certainly, that mother–daughter connection relied on for so long has changed, and a new way of communicating needs to be found. Paul Dillon says dads often have it easier with their daughters than mums. A cup of coffee can equal a connection; there's not the need for deep and meaningful conversations. And while daughters can manipulate their dads expertly, the connection is effortless. Mothers, for a reason no-one seems able to explain, are judged more harshly by their daughters. And unfortunately, says Dillon, some mothers take their daughters down a dangerous path. 'What some mums do for a connection is say, "I'll let them get dressed up like a 25-year-old and let them do what they want." A lot of these girls, who are kind of nightmares, have nightmares of mothers as well. That's the truth,' he says. Parents tell him they worry that if they don't allow their daughter to do things, the daughter will not be liked by others; she'll be socially isolated, without friends. Dillon gives the example of one mother who couldn't understand how her daughter's party went wrong, despite inviting about 300 people. 'Once again, it's young people bullying their parents, or it's parents who want to one-up somebody else.' Others agree, pointing to the party competitiveness that begins before a child goes to school. We all want to do something a bit different – and in some cases, Dillon says, it's meant parents are hiring out commercial theatres for twenty five-year-olds. The expectation grows each year, so can we expect anything less when our daughters turn 14?

The girls are not innocent in this process. Repeatedly experts say they 'bully their parents' into allowing them to do something – but have no idea how to handle things when something goes wrong. 'These are girls who are getting themselves into trouble – getting themselves drunk, ending up in hospital. If you speak to emergency departments, it is very young girls. It's around the 14- and 15-year-old age group – that's when they start seeing them. These are girls who are going out and partying with 16- and 17-year-old boys, who are able to handle their alcohol a little bit better,' Dillon says.

So what should a parent do when a 14-year-old asks to attend a party?

Dillon gives three party rules to help parents. Rule number one. If your child says you 'can't' do something, you simply must. So when your 14-year-old says that you 'can't possibly call the parents who are putting on the party', go ahead and do exactly that. When they claim 'you can't drop me off at the party', make sure that you do. And when they demand that 'you can't pick me up', plan to do that too. Dillon says those arguments, delivered by the girls, are aimed at embarrassing their parents. And often, the girls win out, earning a reprieve. 'Almost every parent can remember their own mum or dad doing something terribly embarrassing when they were young, and I guarantee you promised yourself that you would never do the same thing to your child,' he says. But, if you want to ensure their safety, there's no choice but to call the parents of those putting on the party. Drop-off for a 14-year-old should involve walking her to the door of the house she is visiting and 'damn the potential embarrassment'. 'This ridiculous practice of dropping a 14-year-old off at the end of a driveway and not even watching them go into the house is unbelievably dangerous and borders on child abuse, as far as I'm concerned,' Dillon says. 'Time and time again I hear of parents who do this because they are bullied into it by their child telling them that they will be embarrassing them in front of their friends if they're seen anywhere near the party. Big deal!'

Rule number two. Pick your child up from a party personally, or get someone you trust to pick them up. Dillon says he sees more and more parents who are happy to hand over a wad of cash to their teen to grab a cab home after a party, and teachers are hearing more and more about girls taking Ubers on their own, using their parents' account. 'Sadly, we're seeing Year 10s and even younger who are finding their own way home from these events,' he says. Cab drivers are refusing the pick-ups because of the state some of the youngsters (most often the young women) are in, and fear that due to their age and obvious vulnerability, if they do allow them in the vehicle they could be accused of inappropriate behaviour at a later date. So rule number two, according to Dillon, is that the parent should always make the decision on how their teen gets home from a party – with picking them up always the safest option. 'A few years ago I was commissioned by a school to roll out a survey to students, teachers and parents that examined patterns of alcohol use across all three groups, as well as their attitudes and values around the issue,' he says. Dillon told the principal of the commissioning school that one question she wanted added would not draw a big response, because parents would not be truthful. The question related to the reason they were unlikely to pick up their teen on a Saturday night. 'The response,' says Dillon, 'was staggering.' Of the parents who completed the survey, 'well over one-third of them said that the reason was that they had been drinking themselves.'

Rule number three. Find out as much as you can about the event and don't rely on your teen for that information. Here Dillon makes another terrific point. Just reread the last note from your child's class teacher relating to an upcoming excursion. It goes on and on and on, detailing everything from the method of transport to what your child needs to bring and the possibility of bad weather. Teachers have to do that for a class excursion, but we don't see parents putting the same effort into finding out details of an upcoming party, where more things could go wrong. 'Let's quickly do a comparison,' Dillon says. 'A school excursion for a class of Year 10s to a museum in the middle of the day, and a 15-year-old's birthday party held on a Saturday night for 80–100 of their closest friends – I think it's pretty obvious which one is likely to be the most risky!'

Dillon suggests parents find the answers to these questions:

Whose party is it and how well do you know them?
Where will the party be held?

Will the parents be there and will they be supervising the party?

What time does it start and what time does it finish?

Now that party invitations are regularly posted on social media (including on 'closed' pages), here's a list of other handy questions Dillon suggests:

Is alcohol going to be allowed at the party?

How are the parents going to handle the alcohol issue?

Will an effort be made to stop alcohol being taken into the party?

Will there be security?

The chances are that the party your daughter goes to will be a fabulous celebration of an important milestone. She should be able to enjoy loud music and dance like she's 12. She should be able to relish the glamour and revel in the gossip. But the problem here is the wide variance in how parents deal with this. Some 14-year-olds will arrive by cab, others with friends. Some – but always, say the experts, the minority – will be walked to the door by a parent. As the balloons pop and the music is lowered, parents will still mainly pick up their teens. But some won't. Those girls will hitch a ride with a friend, call a cab, or even decide, on the spot, that she will sleep over at a friend's place. Your daughter is seeing that wide independence given to some of her peers, and wondering why you are so set on embarrassing her by deliberately crawling out of bed at 10 pm, getting dressed, driving 35 minutes across town and collecting her. It's a matter of trust, she might tell you on the way home, and you clearly don't trust her.

That accusation is a tiny price to pay for the knowledge that she is safe.

Success. At what cost?

'*My biggest worry is being a failure.*'

HILLARY,

14

Susan was failing Year 10 Chemistry and Biology when she picked up the phone and dialled Kids Helpline. She was super-stressed and didn't know where else she could go. 'Year 10 can be really tough, hey,' the Kids Helpline counsellor said.

Susan explained how she had tried to turn to others. Her teacher didn't understand, while her mum did – at least she thought she did – but her dad would never. He, in Susan's words, would get really mad and confiscate her iPad. Susan's sister shared the brunt of his expectations; she was recently found crying during a test because of a fear her mark would not be good enough.

Susan feels worse because her friends get all As. She tells the counsellor that she 'feels dumb' beside them. She loves her dad, she adds quickly.

'It's clear that those grades have really affected how you feel about yourself, your relationship with your dad and even with friends. What happens when you feel stressed?' the counsellor asks.

Susan gets depressed. Cries. Finds herself angry for no reason.

The counsellor, skilled at taking these calls – partly because she's taken so many of them – focuses Susan's attention on what makes her feel better.

Skype. Friends. Eating. She says she wants to drop out at the end of the year and work at Kmart.

'It can be very tempting to quit something when it's really difficult to do and when it makes us feel stressed,' the counsellor says. 'The thing about dropping out is that it might avoid the current stress, but life can be stressful sometimes and it's helpful to have strategies you can use to manage the stress when it comes up. Does that make sense?' Susan agrees. The counsellor continues, suggesting a visit to the school guidance officer and coaxing her young client to try exercise – something as simple as a walk – to calm her nerves.

The counsellor will have more than one Susan this afternoon. With exams around the corner, a string of teenagers will be calling for help. Some will want to know how to tell their parents they've not got the grade they expect. Others will plead for assistance in how to alert their parents to the fact that they failed to get an invitation into an academic extension class. Susan might not be your daughter, but she is a growing clientele for school guidance officers, teen psychologists and Kids Helpline.

Alex Curtis, Counselling Centre Supervisor at Kids Helpline, says that doing well at school – sometimes beyond their abilities – has become a serious problem for 14-year-old girls. 'I think academic pressure is a huge issue for young people who call us. They want to do well, they feel pressured to do well.' Sometimes that pressure comes from the school. Other times it comes from their peers. Often, it comes from their parents.

Cath is another example. She first contacted Kids Helpline in January 2016. A new year of school was beckoning for the 14-year-old, and the pressure was mounting each day. She explained how her parents wanted her to be 'the perfect child'. To Cath, that meant perfect grades at school. No Bs. None. Perfect girls don't get substandard marks. The bell hadn't rung to signal the start of the school term, but Cath was confessing to Kids Helpline: she was stressed, anxious; she had started self-harming. It was her way of coping, she explained. It wasn't a big problem, she said. The cuts were superficial and she didn't need medical attention. Cath wanted to know what else she could do to cope.

It's easy to dismiss Susan and Cath as other people's children. Ours are unlike them – we'd know if we were contributing to the stress, we'd know if they were self-harming. But would we? Like every other 14-year-old mentioned in this book, Susan and Cath's names have been changed to protect their identities, but it is unlikely their parents were aware they were in contact with Kids Helpline. These adolescents were articulate, sensible and mature enough to make the decision to seek help. So are so many of the thousands of others who pick up the phone, get online or seek assistance from a counselling service.

Kids Helpline has 120 counsellors working 24 hours a day. The busiest time begins when the school bell closes the day, and teenagers pack up and start heading home. A spike comes about 4 pm. But school hours can be busy too, as children try to navigate the expectations put upon them. 'A lot of the contacts we get are from young females who feel there is a lot of pressure from their parents – whether that is real or perceived, we can't be sure,' Curtis says. But in some cases, it even carries the threat of violence. 'There's kids saying, "I got a C or D on my exam and I don't want to go home because Dad will hit me." There's certainly a lot of real threats.'

Often, counsellors say, it's not the children who struggle at school who are seeking advice but the ones who are studying hard, and who mostly do well. 'Generally, it's the intelligent kids – good kids who feel they must succeed.

They must only get As. If they don't get As then they are going to be in trouble at home.' Others reveal that their big sister or big brother brought home the perfect report card, and nothing less will be accepted by their parents. 'I feel pressure to be as good as my siblings at school and I just can't get their marks. I try,' Rose says. If you could see Rose say that, you'd know she's trying with every ounce of her being. The same goes for Frances: 'Mum and Dad want me to be perfect. Why can't I make mistakes?'

Just think about this. A 14-year-old is walking towards home from the bus stop, talking to a counsellor who is running through small role-plays of what the teen can say to Mum or Dad when they reach their destination in ten minutes' time. More often than not the teen will take the suggestion of penning a letter describing to their parents what they are feeling and how they are drowning in a sea of expectations. Other times, knowing what awaits them at home, the best a teen can do is take the counsellor's advice on how to manage their own anxiety, and hopefully talk to someone at the school who might be able to intervene. Several teachers point to the pressure some of our students with an Asian background are under, and examples are numerous. 'I want to do really well in school because my mum was really good and wants me to do the same. My mum is Asian so [there are] very high expectations,' Jan, 14, says. In a couple of years, some parents will be telling their children to lie about their Year 12 scores, because it brings shame on the family. Now, as punishment – certainly in several cases and irrespective of ethnic origin – some students are being locked out of the house or having their phones removed for weeks as punishment for letting their marks slip.

The teens calling Kids Helpline are weighed down by other problems, too. Mental health concerns. Friend and peer problems. Self-harm concerns. Child abuse. Bullying. The list goes on. The need for our children to contact outside help is staggering, with 14-year-old girls making contact with Kids Helpline 22 232 times over the past four years. In almost half those cases, the child will call for assistance. Other times she'll schedule a web chat, or converse with a counsellor by email. In 35 per cent of cases, it will be the first time the 14-year-old girl has contacted the Kids Helpline. Statistics can be read many ways – hence the old saying 'lies, damned lies and statistics' – but turn those figures upside down and inside out, and whatever way you read them they are staggering.

The anxiety surrounding success – academic, social and ultimately financial – cannot be overstated. The girls feeling this anxiety are from good homes, often from top private schools, whose parents work. They have their own bedrooms, smartphones, and go on regular overseas or interstate holidays. They are flooded with opportunities their parents might have missed out on. A university education will be expected (perhaps their father or mother's alma mater will even have been picked out). They will have been encouraged to grab every opportunity they can, be the best, and use high school as their ticket to a successful adulthood. Doing well at school means a good university, the right course, meeting the right people, a good marriage, a big home, wide travel. Everything. And to many parents, it starts at the desk in their daughter's room. 'I feel like my parents are happy if I try my hardest. But if I don't get a good mark, then they get upset,' Ruth says. Anna says much the same: 'My parents did really well. They aced school. They aced university. I don't think they realise it, but they expect As all the time. And then I get a B+ and they say, "You could have done better here." I don't think I could have. I try really, really hard.'

This is an environment alien to many mothers, who might have been 14 in 1985 or 1990, for example. A sizeable number of their own mothers might not have contemplated going beyond Year 10. Of course, many ventured to Year 12 and some on to university – but for that latter category, they might have been the trailblazers, the first in their families to embark on a higher degree. But talk to the girls and their parents and there's an agreement that the pressure on this group of women, in the 1980s and 1990s, was not the same. 'Being 14 is different to what it was, because when my mum was young she didn't have as much pressure to do well as I do – like she didn't go through uni but she still did well and got us through a private school. So I don't want to let her down,' Penney says. Certainly for Penney and her friends' mothers, there wasn't the same expectation that they finish year 12 and venture on to university. Many of them made that decision for themselves and marched out the gates of their school and into higher education. In February 1985, according to the Australian Bureau of Statistics, women made up 38 per cent of the total workforce, a jump on previous years. And that has continued to grow. In 1990 it was 41 per cent and last year, in 2016, women comprised 46 per cent of the workforce.[1] They are accountants and lawyers and administrators, specialists and policy experts and academics. Many of these mothers now have 14-year-old girls, and their expectations are that their daughters will also finish their education at a university. Many of them have worked hard and long, forgoing an overseas trip or a house upgrade, so that their daughters have that opportunity. But all of this brings an expectation that many of the girls are floundering under. Listen to a group of 14-year-old girls mimic their mothers and it goes like this: 'I work so you can go to a good school', or 'I didn't have the opportunities I'm giving you, so work harder.' 'My mum is never angry,' Tricia says, 'she's just disappointed. That's what she says. That really gets to me.' Tricia's comment leads to a chorus of 'me too'. It's not that the girls don't appreciate what has been given to them, but they feel an enormous burden to succeed at school, and beyond, or fail in the eyes of their parents – particularly their mothers. Associate Professor Alan Ralph says with both parents working, their daughters were afforded greater opportunities. 'But if a teenager says, I don't want what you are trying to get me to do, and the parent says, I'm sacrificing everything in order to give you all the things I never had – that's a recipe for an argument if ever I saw one.'

In my class, in rural Queensland, fewer than a handful of girls attended a big-city university. Most of my friends, at the university college where country kids seemed to stay, were in the same boat. Of course there were exceptions, but in most cases our mothers didn't work outside the home. If they did, they volunteered. They wanted us to live full and happy lives, but that didn't automatically include a demand that we top our class, get the right university degree and embark on a speedy career trajectory. Often it involved finishing Year 10 or 12 and finding a solid job that would provide the foundation to save. The local bank was always a favourite; a good employer who was unlikely to close down and where kids could learn customer service and the importance of money.

My educational path might have even been less pressured than most. Both my parents were initially opposed to their daughter being university educated. It was a step too far, in their minds. School was for learning, and fun, and meeting people and setting myself up for a solid post-school job. Afternoon tea was ready each day when the five of us children lumbered home: a pavlova, or a fresh chocolate cake. Chores. Play. A bath. And fitting your homework somewhere in between. Extracurricular activities like basketball or ballet or speech and drama might take up one afternoon, but rarely more than that. In their minds, I would probably stay in the small town I called home, marry someone local and have a fulfilled life. It was me, at the urging of a teacher, who persuaded my parents to let me leave town and venture to university – a path no-one else in the family had trodden at that stage.

In 2017, that seems incredibly old-fashioned, but many families today, particularly from rural areas, have a similar story. My friend, brought up at the beach, spent long summer afternoons surfing, not studying. I look at my friends now, as a focus group. A couple of them boasted mothers who pushed them to study hard. Some of them urged their children to aim for a teaching degree (a good profession where they could have the school holidays free). But most of them mirrored my case: do your best; life is the total of much more than your 12 years of school; success is a good marriage and a good family, good health and good friends.

Fast-forward 30 years and it is a different story. I work. So do almost all of those friends I mentioned, whose mothers didn't. We all went to university; indeed, we met there. We all have our own children now. And what are our expectations? We have worked to give our sons and daughters opportunities. Expensive schools. Holiday camps. Maths clubs. Gymnasium competitions. Cooking courses. And mostly, even if we don't want to admit it, we want them to do really well in all of them. We wear a good school report as a badge of pride; we provided the environment – even put a desk in their bedroom – and the encouragement for them to do well. We glow when they are plucked out of the pack and sent to the extension course for Maths or English or Science or Coding. Our expectation as to how our girls will compete with boys is that they will of course rise to the same level. We've given our children every opportunity to make the path through life as easy as we can, and that started with a good school education. In other words, we have skin in the game.

Most principals and teachers understand that, because they've worn the parent hat too. Take Flo Kearney, the former head of Brisbane's Somerville House, as an example. Her daughters are now in their 20s, but she admits while she – one of seven children – was not pressured to pursue university by her parents, her daughters understood, from an early age, that they were expected to follow her into tertiary education. 'It's just part of the way we've brought up our girls,' she says. Was pressure exerted on them? 'Yes,' she says honestly. Kearney adds another important element here. Parents who choose to send their girls to a single-sex school are looking for a particular education. 'We are saying – and I certainly do believe – that it's better for young women to be educated in an all-girls' environment because of the way they flourish, the way they feel safe, the way that they will try anything because that's the expectation. However, the other side of that is that there is probably more expectation on girls in all-girls' schools because of that underlying factor – they've been given the opportunity to have a different education where young women are stretched and expected to really achieve what they are capable of achieving, to the best that they can be.' That's an important double-edged sword. 'Some girls absolutely thrive and others find the expectation too much,' Kearney says. The latter is the cohort that struggle with emotional problems, require counselling and, often, other interventions.

Social researcher Mark McCrindle calls it 'expectation inflation': where one in four Generation Xers had a university degree, the ratio for this current generation of 14-year-olds will be one in two. McCrindle says parents sacrifice much to get children to university, and that has placed unintended expectations on our Generation Zs. 'It has brought us that term – the quarter-life crisis – so we might see more of that with Gen Z,' he says. That might mean that some of our 14-year-olds, by the time they reach their mid 20s, will wither under the angst of not yet starting a multi-million dollar business or launching a new smart-device app. 'There's always been success but it wasn't as in your face,' McCrindle says. 'Now everyone's watching the highlight reel of everyone else on Facebook, or through friends. It can be constant ... a "sense of everyone's doing stuff and you're not", and so it can create [feelings of] inadequacy.'

Jody Forbes, Brisbane Girls' Grammar School psychologist, talks about the state known as 'Rushing Women's Syndrome'. She describes it as women who run themselves ragged with a never-ending list of tasks – 'those who frequently answer "stressed" or "busy" to friends' questions about their welfare, when a trip to the dentist becomes the only opportunity to sit still and abstain from talking, when coffee becomes akin to religion and when sleep is hard to come by.' After fighting to win the prize of equality, it's a bit like these women are having to prove it every day. 'It's like we have to do everything. "I have to work. I have to be a great mother. I have to be a great neighbour." Some days I'd like to stay at home in an apron ... We are told we can do anything, but do we have to do everything at once?' Forbes says one of the proven remedies for both the frantic, super-hero mothers and their frenetic daughters, is 'mindfulness' – something her school is now teaching its students, mirroring other organisations like Google, universities and schools, hospitals, banks and even the United States Marines.

Evaluated positively by both the University of Cambridge and Oxford Brookes University, Brisbane Girls' Grammar School uses the .b (dot-be) program, which stands for Stop, Breathe and Be. 'The lifestyle at the moment for parents and their children is so busy that we don't stop,' Forbes says. 'I have to make a concerted effort to sit down at the dinner table – and we know how much research there is to show that families that sit down together at the dinner table have a lot of good outcomes.' Think for a moment of the last time your whole family ate together, over dinner. Even with the best of intentions, frequently, with the push for us all to be better, fitter and wiser, life intervenes. Swimming lessons after school Monday. Violin on Tuesday. Netball practice on Wednesday. Thursday is the dentist/doctor/physiotherapy/tax appointment. Sometimes, we forget to just stop and sit down. 'We have to actually teach kids that,' Forbes says. 'We need our adolescents to experience boredom. That is not a bad thing.'

Recently, ahead of a national girls' education conference, Brisbane Girls' Grammar School filmed their students both during a lesson in mindfulness, and in a hallway immediately after the lesson. 'You could actually see the difference,' Forbes says. 'They were at peace. Smiling.' She says many studies have shown the benefits of pausing. These range from a reduction in stress, anxiety, exhaustion and depression, to improvements in concentration, visual–spatial memory and creativity. Other schools have other programs, with yoga being a popular inclusion. At the end of those classes, the yoga teacher will often have to go and wake up several students, the chance to relax having quickly sent them to sleep.

Ask teachers whether many parents are pushing their children too far and they'll nod, telling stories of parents questioning half-marks on big assignments, demanding re-marking, and even withdrawing their children because they didn't receive the mark the parents expected. 'We have parents on the phone constantly,' one Victorian teacher says. She tells the story of one father who called, half-screaming, half-crying. 'You'd think someone had died – and then it turned out his daughter had missed out on something. His daughter was fine, it's just that her performance fell short of his expectations.' A Queensland teacher nominates dealing with parents as 'the most time-consuming element of our day'. 'The girls are so easy – but our counsellors and our teachers and our principal are exhausted. Parents are the real problem.' And the pressure being applied is not just to do well academically, it is the pressure to win, to be the best. 'My biggest pressure is to get into the eight for rowing,' Sally explains. 'Also to stay on top of my work, because I used to be good at school but not as much now.' And Phoebe: 'I have to get up early and go for a run, do weights because I want to get into the eight in rowing. Dad is the rowing coach. He expects me [to be] in it.'

Clinical psychologist Dr Judith Locke, who wrote *The Bonsai Child*, says parents have to learn to step back sufficiently for their daughters to step up, and living through disappointments helps a teenager's development. She says parents might have the best intentions, but were actually limiting their children in a bid to provide them with perfect childhoods. Many even made decisions – like working two jobs, or where they lived and what school their children attended – to make life as 'perfect' for their child as they could. 'But with that comes a whole range of problems, because we are so intent on giving them these perfect lives that they come out of it unprepared for the world,' Locke says. 'We give them such a sheltered existence and perfect conditions ... they get very much caught up in expecting things to go well for them all time.' Parents, instead of just focusing on self-esteem to make their daughter feel better, needed to teach them three vital skills of resourcefulness, resilience and self-regulation.

Remember when you were young, authority was rarely questioned. The local police officer was beyond reproach. Your GP was unquestionably correct. And the school teacher was the pillar of our local suburbs and communities. Now, as private school fees chew into family finances, parents want a greater say. Consequently, teachers are fair game. I ask one teacher whether she wants her own daughter to be the top of the class. Her answer is brutally honest: 'Part of me does. I wasn't private-school educated. This is our first private school. Tanya has always got an A for English. She's never been the big star but she's always got As and Bs. Now she's getting a C for English and Science, and I was [thinking], "Oh my God, what is going on?"' It's been a hard lesson. 'She fancies herself as a singer but didn't get into the encore group. She's played netball for seven years and been in Division 1 and Division 2, but now has barely scraped into the C team.' She says she understands how other parents feel, but what they all need to remember is how their daughter is feeling. 'My daughter couldn't care less she got a C in English. She's happy. She's got friends. She's having a ball. I'm the one who cared about the C, and I've got to contain that.' Parents as well as students have to learn to manage expectations.

It's not only the 'professionalisation of mothers', as one teacher put it, that has placed a burden on their teen daughters; the education system has added to it. 'School, academically, is harder,' says Jody Forbes. She points to a challenging national curriculum, increased competition for university spaces, NAPLAN exams and the MySchools websites as contributing to the stress many students face. She points also to Mission Australia's annual Youth Survey. While it targets 15- to 19-year-old teens, Forbes says the top three issues of concern – 18 994 young people were surveyed in 2015 – rarely changes between years. Coping with stress topped last year's area of concern, with

38.4 per cent indicating that they were either extremely concerned or very concerned. School or study problems featured as a second major concern, and body image as a third (33.6 per cent and 26.5 per cent respectively).[2]

A boon in academic extension courses has also increased tension. Rare when many of these girls' parents went to high school, they are now offered across most schools. English extension for those who are performing above their class level. Special Maths clubs and national competitions for those who show a flair there. Science meetings at lunchtime. Early university invitations for the special few. Those who are selected are acknowledged in class assemblies and in school newsletters. They're seen by their peers as the stars in the class; the ones who are at the front of the pack. That puts pressure not only on those girls not chosen – 'it means I have to try harder' – but also on those chosen. The competition is tougher. The odds are higher. A big fish in a small sea becomes a big fish in a big sea. Their expectations grow, along with the expectations of their parents. 'I would say the calls we get from young girls who are struggling with pressure at school to succeed academically are either from schools that have academic programs or from private schools,' Alex Curtis from Kids Helpline says. And then there's the 'my parents are paying for me to go to this school and I feel I have to do well'. Says Bridget, 14: 'My family has done quite well and I want to live up to that and make them proud. I want to be better than my cousins.'

Maggie Dent, educator, author and parenting guru, hears that regularly now but admits it was something she never – or rarely – heard when she worked as a teacher. In between children, Dent taught high school English, Drama and Physical Education from 1977 to 1998 in various Western Australian schools. 'What we're saying to our kids is that my capacity to love you is determined by how good you make me look as a parent. We all want the best we can for our children. But they see it as, you will only love me if . . . That's not what the parent is saying.'

Julie Warwick is the savvy head of Robina State High School on the Gold Coast, a big co-ed school with 1400 students. 'We have to keep trying to espouse that message around doing the best you can, recognising effort as opposed to achievement,' she says. Parents and teachers needed to encourage positive behaviour. Students needed to set goals. Both cohorts needed to be realistic. 'I have to do that with my parent hat on as well,' Warwick says.

Denise, a 14-year-old student, says teachers add to the pressure by drilling into Year 9 students that their marks in that year will determine how well they do in Year 12. 'It's three years away. That's just not fair,' she says. And Caitlyn says, 'They expect me to know now what I'm going to be in ten years' time. How do I know?' Sometimes, peers add to the burden of pressure already weighing down on a student. 'The kids I hang out with are really smart and I am happy with my mark, and then they tell me their mark and I feel bad because mine isn't as good as that,' Sarah says.

These girls are desperate for their parents to understand that, mostly, they are giving it their all. They are not skiving off, skipping class or failing to do their homework. It's just that the competition is intense; they're pitted against their friends, and sometimes they come up short – at least in their parents' view. Tina says her goal is to be 'a doctor and a mum later'. But she is desperate for her mum to understand that she can't try any harder. I ask her what she wants to tell her mother. Her answer: 'It's okay to not do well sometimes.' Tina says she hopes her mother reads that comment here, and knows in her heart it's from her daughter. Narelle is sitting next to her. She adds her own expression of hope: 'I will be closer to my child so I'll know how she feels.'

Mothers and daughters

'No-one could ever replace you as my
mother. I would do anything for you.'

SIENA,

8

'I love my mother and everything,
but it's not cool to say that.'

AUGUSTA,

14

Those Hallmark cards have nothing on the treasured
stash of home-made greetings mothers receive from
their young daughters. Dive back through them, and
you're guaranteed a broad smile. We are their all, early on:
their defender, their keeper of secrets and their inspiration.
We can do no wrong, as they copy our walk and our talk
and follow us into the toilet, just to be with us. One of

my favourite Mother's Day gifts was a book of home-made vouchers – I received one from both my daughters when they were aged about seven and eight. Each voucher entitled me to the sweet treats I'd obviously yearned for, at that time. Daily hugs, kisses, back rubs, quiet time, even being allowed to go to the toilet by myself. They were all promised, in a little book, stapled together by a child. Their genius was the promise that they'd never run out. I know they will.

Most teen girls – and more often than not it's around that sticky age of 13 and 14 – will see their mother through another prism. They will no longer see her as their defender, they'll choose to share their secrets with their friends, and home will not muster up an iota of inspiration. In your daughter's mind, she is being consistent; it's you who has changed. Overnight, she might even come to the conclusion that you are hell-bent on ruining her life. 'You are the worst mother in the world,' she may shout as the door slams on her bedroom. 'You couldn't possibly understand how I feel.' 'You don't trust me.' Or even, 'Why can't you be like the other mothers? I wish I had one of them.' Home becomes a theatre, and mothers find themselves starring as the villain in a daily drama.

The mother–daughter relationship is as unique as it is wondrous, and no matter how bumpy those teenage years can be, it's a union that is almost always built for life. Sometimes, within months of your relationship having been turned on its head, your kind, open daughter will return through the front door. Other times, it might take years. But usually, by the time she has her own child, she will be knocking on the door with an understanding of a mother, herself. Once again you will become her best defender, the keeper of her secrets and the font of wisdom. Associate Professor Alan Ralph, from the Triple P Positive Parenting Program, says a rough calculation exists as to how long your daughter might spend in that teenhood tunnel away from you, and much of it depended on how parents handled those tricky teen years. The more parents reacted against their teens, the longer the journey through the tunnel was likely to last.

Ralph often uses an earthquake analogy when he's talking to the parents of teens. 'Raising kids, particularly teenagers, is like living in an earthquake zone,' he says. 'You've got the kids pushing one way, wanting more freedom, and you've got the parent who has traditionally resisted that.' That means, over time, tension simmers and builds. 'Every so often there's a little earthquake,' Ralph says. 'The parents give a little bit, and the teens get a little bit and there's a bit of wobbliness for a day or two and then it all settles down.' It also means the ground shifts slightly, as new parameters build and parents acknowledge their teens' growing maturity. 'But if parents dig their heels in and stick to it, it's a bit like living in a pressure cooker, because if you don't allow those little shifts to occur in a graduated and managed way, at some point you're going to get the big one. And that can be so destructive.' Ralph has seen families break down at this point, and the teens leave home.

This is especially the case in the relationship between mothers and daughters because, despite the push for more parental involvement by fathers – and it has grown in leaps and bounds over recent years – mothers remain, largely, the chief parent. You just need to visit a parenting night to see that: the audience is overwhelmingly comprised of women. Those who run parent training courses say the same. In the early years of raising children, it is predominantly women who outlay the enormous investment of time and effort that is required, often forgoing their own promising careers to do so. Moulding their child into a good person becomes part of who they are, a daily goal that they don't hand over when the child becomes an adolescent. Dr Judith Locke, author of *The Bonsai Child*, says she remembers once seeing a mug for sale with 'A Daughter is a Mother's Best Friend' written on it. 'That idea of you being a twosome is really pushed,' she says. But that makes it very hard for your daughter to separate from you without it looking like a slap across the face. As a student counsellor, Locke used to notice some mothers getting jealous of their daughter's friends. Why? Because they could see their daughter was giving to her friends those moments that used to be given to her. She says too often children have adult rights but child responsibilities; they might be out at the movies or a party and their mother will be at home doing their washing. 'As your child becomes more independent, you have to as well,' she says. 'When your child starts to choose a Saturday night with their friends, you need to start choosing Saturday night with your friends as well.'

Not that any of that is easy. Teens don't suddenly wake up when they are 15 or 16 full of worldly wisdom; that is acquired gradually – as it was with us – through experiences with the outside world. Our role, as parents, is to give them the skills to be able to do that. Marise McConaghy, principal of Strathcona Baptist Girls' Grammar School in Melbourne, says research shows that arguments might be a crucial part of the relationship between mother and daughter. She points to Terri Apter's book *You Don't Really Know Me: Why Mothers and Daughters Fight and How Both Can Win*, where mothers are asked to remember their own teenage years and the relationship they had with their mothers. Rather than viewing teenage rebellion as an attempt to leave one's mother, Apter sees it as an attempt by daughters to relate to their mothers in new ways by making their mothers see them as the young adults they want to be. She says that daughters are not trying to make their mothers crazy or to reject them, but instead are trying hard to define themselves through words and actions. Apter says it's worth remembering that it takes two to argue. 'Mothers get heated because they may see their daughter as trying to push them away, so the misconception about the conflict actually increases the conflict,' she told me. 'Or, a mother herself may feel confused and even threatened when a daughter says, "You don't really know me!" That is a harsh relational challenge, and may lead a mother to worry that her "ignorance" of who the daughter is means that she lacks influence, that her daughter is out of control, and may put herself at risk. The daughter's challenge is to persuade her mother that who she "really is" (or wants to be, or is becoming) is a strong woman who can be trusted to look after her own best interests.' And her advice? All this takes time!

But based on Apter's thesis, arguing can be seen as a process by which your daughter builds new connections with you. 'Even if it seems as if she's picking a fight for no other reason than to pick a fight, it is often really because she's feeling anxious about something she can't articulate,' McConaghy says. 'A fight allows her to get it out into the open. Ideally, your response will allow her to gain insight into her own feelings and to reach her own safe, healthy conclusions. That's less likely to happen if you jump in too quickly with advice, or if either of you get even a whiff of defensiveness, anger, judgement or dismissal. If you can somehow manage not to take the argument personally, both of you may be able to hear some very important information.'

That means, as mothers, we need to look for opportunities to give a little and allow our teen girls to mature alongside it. That's easy on some days, but as so many mothers pointed out to me, what do you do when your teen adopts a standpoint, just for the sake of it, or worse, to get a rise? According to Ralph, that too is a normal part of growing up. 'How do kids rebel? How do they separate themselves from their parents' generation? When I was growing up in the '60s it was drugs, rock and roll and sex, and it was easy. Now with parents who have had that, how do the kids rebel against that? What I see as the area of rebelling is piercing and tattoos. That seems to be the one area that our generation didn't embrace, unless you come from a particular culture like New Zealand.' Ralph says research shows that, in adult life, our children tend to come back to where their parents' values sat. 'If you know that, at least you have a sense of "it will come right in the end",' he says. Mia Freedman says that this might be the first generation that's had to parent in a world they don't understand. 'When we were teenagers, what did we do? We snuck out, we wore our skirts shorter than our parents wanted us to, we were on the phone too much, we listened to music that our parents thought was annoying or inappropriate. They were all the exact same things that our parents did when they were teenagers.

But you now have a whole landscape in the digital world that is like a foreign language. It's completely unknown to parents, and they don't know how to make the rules because they don't understand the game. Most parents do not even understand what their kids are talking about. They're panicked because they don't know how to keep them safe and they don't know how to teach them digital hygiene in the same way that they teach them road safety or basic nutrition or all of those things.'

Freedman, a former women's magazine editor, says a teen girl's biggest role model is always her mother; a claim proved each time magazines like *Dolly* surveyed the issue. Says Freedman, 'Women and girls are always looking to the next phase of life and they are always looking at women and girls who are that little bit further down the road than them so they can learn about what their life is going to be like in a few years. Young girls are the same. They have a living, breathing role model in their house and in their life 24/7. How can you be anything other than the main role model?' That doesn't necessarily mean they want to be like us, but they are looking to us to decide who they want to be. And pushing up against us is all part of them seeking their own identity. 'My daughter said to me the other day, when I was kind of nagging her to go shopping with me, "Mum, I'm different to you. I don't like shopping." I thought, "That's interesting." [She was] really putting a stake in the ground and saying, "I am a different person to you. I'm not mini-you."'

The crucial point is not to try to force our daughters to mirror us. The more parents react against their children's views, the more likely it is that the teens will dig their heels in. In Ralph's parlance, there'll be an earthquake warning. The second factor here is that when teens are seeking independence and considering ideas and values that might be the polar opposite to those to their parents, they need a safe place to explore them. Is school the best place to do that? Probably not – what about inside their friendship circles? Probably not – they might be humiliated or ostracised for thinking outside the square. Home, experts say, should be that safe place where teens feel secure in arguing their view. And the universal advice is to take it at face value. If your teen wants to run off and join a cult, be curious. Ask, why? What's the process? What're the consequences? More often than not your child will consider the answers to those questions and they'll decide home isn't such a bad place after all.

What's hard, for many mothers, is the acceptance that the relationship between mother and daughter must change. Those childhood ties have to give way to adulthood. Physically, she is growing into a woman. Biologically, she is becoming a sexual adult. Psychologically, she is working out who she is, and where she sits in a big world, outside her family. 'Ask any mother of daughters and she will say that the only thing tougher than being an adolescent girl is being her mother,' Marise McConaghy told the Strathcona mothers of Year 12s. 'Ask any daughter and she will say that adolescence is the time she most wants her mother emotionally, but is also most resistant to this need.'

That's true. That's exactly what the 14-year-olds I asked told me. Almost unanimously they said they wanted a close relationship with their mother. 'She just kind of goes all child and family psychologist on me,' says Anthea. 'She just doesn't understand and we both end up yelling,' says Beth. Some of them acknowledge that they are lucky enough to call their union close. 'My mum always knows what to say and I trust her unconditionally,' Sue says. 'I talk to Mum all the time because she makes me feel better,' Lucia says. But many of them yearn for a closer relationship, even to the point of contacting Kids Helpline in seeking it. 'She's just too busy,' says Karen. Alex says her relationship with her mother has taught her how she will parent a teen girl. 'I'll try as hard as possible to let her say exactly what she is feeling and allow her to say whatever she wants and talk about anything with me,' she says. And Samantha: 'I'll make sure I talk to her and make sure everything is okay at school and home.'

Perhaps intriguingly, most girls, despite being so articulate, don't know how to seek that relationship. They don't want to be the little girl who handed over the schmaltzy Mother's Day cards, and wasn't it their mother's job to improve their relationship anyway? 'For both mother and daughter then, adolescence and young adulthood is a time when the potential for feeling lonely, confused, misunderstood and hurt by the other may be at its peak,' McConaghy says. 'The adolescent girl is going through a complex and important process vital to her development and capacity to flourish in the world. However, it is more confusing because where she is in this process slides backwards and forwards, and in one day your breath might be taken away by her maturity, integrity and thoughtfulness and the next by disappointment in her childish selfishness and self-indulgence. Also, she can be hard to read and difficult to trust because she may be completely honest and transparent about some matters, yet feel that it is morally acceptable to deceive and dissemble about other matters, such as the level of parental supervision at 'gatherings', or where she actually was for the duration of a Saturday-night outing.' Sound familiar?

Fran Reddan, principal of Mentone Girls' Grammar School in Victoria, describes an analogy she heard somewhere, that a girl's mother becomes a bit like the edge of a swimming pool during her daughter's adolescence. 'The girl goes and swims out and tries things and then comes back to the side – that is her mum – to catch her breath. Then when she kicks away, it is like a kick to Mum.' It's the perfect analogy. 'I feel for the mums,' Reddan says. 'I really feel that the relationship between a girl and her mum at that particular stage gets really tough, because they [the girls] know how to push buttons.' An unusual and unfamiliar creature walks out of the bedroom inhabited only a few years ago by their 'lovely, uninhibited, gorgeous angel of a 10-year-old', she says.

No doubt exists, though, that a mother's investment in the relationship she has with her daughter is the best investment she can make. But it's also a high-stakes investment – arguably more than for previous generations. Families are choosing to have fewer children, so the time that used to be spread across six or seven or eight siblings years ago, is now focused on one or two. Add a couple of other ingredients – those opportunities a mother might have missed in her own childhood, or the goals she holds for her precious daughter – and the urge to keep control of the puppet strings can be overwhelming. So too can the feeling of guilt. Perhaps you missed a school sports day, or arrived late for your daughter's violin performance? A new dress might be the solution. Is that so bad? Experts responded with an 'it depends'. It appears it comes down to our own motivation. 'Perhaps it's a case of we do it because we can,' one expert said. But it's also possible that we're doing it because 'we think we should'.

Alan Ralph raises another issue here that might highlight a difference between our daughters' lives and those of our grandmothers. Once upon a time, in big families, horizontal relationships developed easily. Siblings would help each other; sisters might end up also being best friends. Now, with fewer children, those horizontal relationships are changing. 'We're seeing a vertical relationship between grandmothers and mothers and daughters because there is no-one horizontally,' Ralph says. The girls point to that, too. Although some of them certainly still rely on their big sisters for advice, many of them are cared for by their grandparents, because their mothers and fathers are at work.

At a big parenting night in Brisbane, put on by local MP Di Farmer, Ralph holds the stage. The audience is made up of parents; probably 90 per cent of them are mothers, and the questions are mostly what Ralph expects. Sibling arguments and social media are both high on the priority list. But the umbrella issue, Ralph sees, is a concern by parents about how to prepare their children for the future. 'It used to be the case that you got a good education, you got a good job, you stayed in that job for 20 or 30 years and you worked your way up the ranks ... that's gone. What is it that parents need to teach their kids, and where do they get it from?' He says while evidence has shown that what you do when your child is a toddler is vital, there's another set of evidence around the ages of 11, 12 and 13 that provides parents with further opportunities. He tells his audiences to be clear about the values they have, and find ways to imbue them in your teens; to have clear expectations and rules (making sure they are reasonable); and to make friends with your teen's friends' parents. This latter piece of advice no-one else has offered along the way of my research. Later, he tells me that often parents become isolated from other parents of kids the same age. 'At primary school it is easy: you meet in the pick-up line, you probably even live in the same area.' That's true. Once our children go to high school, they make their own way to and from schools, and their friends might live, geographically, a world away. That means the ability to connect with other mothers going through the same parenting period is diminished. And, according to Ralph, that can provide the teens with a winning advantage. 'That puts you at a disadvantage, because one of the standard mantras that teens adopt when they're trying to get parents to let them do something is, "All my friends are doing that."' Having contact with other parents, with children the same age allows you to check that.

With so much invested in our daughters, sometimes the pull as mothers to be their friends, not their parents, is strong. Everyone I talked to labelled that a bad idea, mainly because it changes the relationship. First, it's harder to set boundaries and rules. 'If you've got that goal of wanting to be a friend, it can impact quite dramatically on your capacity to act as a parent in setting those boundaries,' Ralph says. It can also set up conflict between parents if the father wants to enforce those boundaries. Marise

McConaghy tells mothers that the role of being a parent is far more precious than trying to be their friend. 'You will always be her mother, her first love and her earliest and most important attachment figure, and nothing, not even adolescence, can take that away from you,' she says. 'Of course, she has to go through adolescence, just as you did, and you both have to survive it. She has to reject you, quietly or not, and you have to survive that rejection. She has to become separate and independent and so she has to become disillusioned with you as the centre of her world, and you have to allow her to do that. She has to know that you are not perfect, because she certainly knows that she is not, and how can she grow up if she thinks that this necessitates perfection? She has to become critical of you to prove to herself that she is "not you", and you have to let her.'

Caroline Paul, the US author of *The Gutsy Girl, Escapades for Your Life of Epic Adventure*, says studies show daughters are being parented differently from sons, and that's something mothers need to be keenly aware of. 'I think without a doubt that women are transferring caution and fear to their daughters,' she says. More effort had to be given to providing the girl with the language of bravery. Paul's comments made me think, immediately, of a terrific TED talk delivered by Reshma Saujani, titled 'Teach girls bravery, not perfection'. Reshma talks about her decision to run for the US Congress. 'For years, I had existed safely behind the scenes in politics as a fundraiser, as an organiser, but in my heart I always wanted to run,' she says in her talk. 'My pollsters told me that I was crazy to run, that there was no way that I could win.' She ran anyway, and ended up feeling humiliated. 'I only got 19 per cent of the vote, and the same papers that said I was a rising political star now said I wasted $1.3 million on 6321 votes. Don't do the math. It was humiliating.' But she says at the age of 33, it was the first time she had done something 'truly brave' where her determination was not to be perfect. 'Most girls are taught to avoid risk and failure. We're taught to smile pretty, play it safe, get all As. Boys, on the other hand, are taught to play rough, swing high, crawl to the top of the monkey bars and then just jump off headfirst. And by the time they're adults, whether they're negotiating a raise or even asking someone out on a date, they're habituated to take risk after risk. They're rewarded for it. It's often said in Silicon Valley, no-one even takes you seriously unless you've had two failed start-ups.' In other words, she says, 'we're raising our girls to be perfect, and we're raising our boys to be brave.'[1]

So in the same year as her attempt to run for Congress – 2012 – Reshma started a company to teach girls to code, which can be painstaking and challenging, where a full stop can mark the difference between something working and something failing. It requires persistence, determination and patience, and often success only comes after failure. She found that girls wouldn't show the progress of their work, unless it was right. It was, in her words, 'perfection or bust'. 'We have to begin to undo the socialisation of perfection, but we've got to combine it with building a sisterhood that lets girls know that they are not alone,' Reshma says.

Perhaps the most common piece of advice I received in the research for this chapter was that, as mothers, we shouldn't take our daughters' 14-year-old interactions with us personally. Sometimes we need to bite our tongue, but keep the communication lines open. Our daughters, on some days, are struggling to know where they are headed next. It's as confusing for them as it is concerning for us. Perhaps that makes it an adventure? 'No matter how many daughters you have,' Marise McConaghy says, 'you have never had this adolescent girl before, which means you are both in uncharted territory, so try to set up an environment which allows both of you to proceed with caution.'

Endnotes

Chapter 2

1 Influence Central, 'Kids & Tech': http://influence-central.com/
kids-tech-the-evolution-of-todays-digital-natives/
2 'Steven Fry "Quits" Twitter over Bafta jibe', *BBC
News*, 15 February 2016: http://www.bbc.com/news/
entertainment-arts-35577913
3 Crockett, E, 'How Twitter Taught a Robot to Hate', Vox,
24 March 2016: http://www.vox.com/2016/3/24/11299034/
twitter-microsoft-tay-robot-hate-racist-sexist
4 Demos, 'New Demos study reveals scale of social media
misogyny': http://www.demos.co.uk/press-release/staggering-
scale-of-socialmedia-misogyny-mapped-in-new-demos-study/

Chapter 3

1 Wahlstrom, K, 'Examining the Impact of Later High School
Start Times on the Health and Academic Performance of
High School Students: A Multi-Site Study', Centre for Applied
Research and Educational Improvement, February 2014:
http://www.spps.org/cms/lib010/MN01910242/Centricity/
Domain/7352/final_version_3-11-14_start_time_report.pdf

2 Belvedere, MJ, 'Why Aetna's CEO pays workers up to $500 to sleep', CNBC, 5 April 2016: http://www.cnbc.com/2016/04/05/why-aetnas-ceo-pays-workers-up-to-500-to-sleep.html

Chapter 4

1 Heritage Bank Money Saving Tips: https://www.heritage.com.au/blog/money-saving-tips/

2 Australian Institute of Family Studies, 'The housework and homework habits of Australian ten and eleven year-olds', 13 July 2012: https://aifs.gov.au/media-releases/housework-and-homework-habits-australian-ten-and-eleven-year-olds

3 University of Melbourne, *The Household, Income and Labour Dynamics in Australia Survey 2016*, 'Selected Findings from Waves 1 to 14': https://www.melbourneinstitute.com/downloads/hilda/Stat_Report/statreport_2016.pdf

Chapter 5

1 Fuller, A and Wicking, A, 'What 91,369 young people can tell us about resilience?', Resilient Youth Australia, 2016.

Chapter 7

1 Rosenman, D, Facebook, 22 November 2015: https://www.facebook.com/davidrosenman/posts/10205305292687547

2 ABS Census Data, 2011 Census QuickStats – family composition: http://www.censusdata.abs.gov.au/census_services/getproduct/census/2011/quickstat/0?opendocument&navpos=220#familycomposition

Chapter 8

1 Miller, D and Funnell, N, *Loveability: An Empowered Girl's Guide to Dating and Relationships*, HarperCollins, Sydney, 2014, p. 32.

2 PR Newswire, 'Self-esteem issues impact women's future success', 31 March 2012: http://www.prnewswire.com/news-releases/self-esteem-issues-impact-womens-future-success-145443215.html

3 Smith, A, et al, Australian Study of Health and Relationships (Number 2): http://www.ashr.edu.au

Chapter 9

1 American Psychological Association, Task Force on the Sexualization of Girls, 'Report of the APA Task Force on the Sexualization of Girls', 2007: http://www.apa.org/pi/women/programs/girls/report-full.pdf

2 'Letting Children be Children, Report of an Independent Review of the Commercialisation and Sexualisation of Childhood', Presented to UK Parliament by the Secretary of State for Education, June 2011: https://www.gov.uk/government/uploads/system/uploads/attachment_data/file/175418/Bailey_Review.pdf

Chapter 10

1 Sax, L, 'Why Do Girls Tend To Have More Anxiety Than Boys?', *New York Times*, 21 April 2016: http://well.blogs.nytimes.com/2016/04/21/why-do-girls-have-more-anxiety-than-boys/?_r=1

2 Patton, GC, et al, 'The prognosis of common mental disorders in adolescents: a 14-year prospective cohort study', *The Lancet*, Volume 383, No. 9926, p1404–1411, 19 April 2014: http://www.thelancet.com/journals/lancet/article/PIIS0140-6736(13)62116-9/fulltext

3 Hinshaw, S, *The Triple Bind*, Ballantine Books, New York, 2009, p 7.

Chapter 11

1 Miller and Funnell, *Loveability*, op cit., p 32.

2 Orenstein, P, *Girls & Sex, Navigating the Complicated New Landscape*, HarperCollins, New York, 2016, p 3.

3 Lang, K, 'Famous women are often slut shamed, but rarely are the men they associate with' *Sunday Mail*, November 15, 2015.

4 Smith, A, et al, Australian Study of Health and Relationships (Number 2): http://www.ashr.edu.au

5 La Trobe University, Teen Sexual Health Survey 2014: http://www.latrobe.edu.au/news/articles/2014/release/teen-sexual-health-survey-launched

Chapter 12

1. National Drug Strategy, 'Australian secondary school students' use of tobacco in 2014': http://www.nationaldrugstrategy. gov.au/internet/drugstrategy/Publishing.nsf/content/BCBF-6B2C638E1202CA257ACD0020E35C/$File/Tobacco%20 Report%202014.PDF

2. National Drug Strategy, 'Australian secondary school students' use of tobacco, alcohol, and over-the-counter and illicit substances in 2011': http://www.nationaldrugstrategy. gov.au/internet/drugstrategy/Publishing.nsf/content/BCBF-6B2C638E1202CA257ACD0020E35C/$File/National%20 Report_FINAL_ASSAD_7.12.pdf

Chapter 13

1. Australian Bureau of Statistics, 'Labour Force, Australia, Detailed, Quarterly', February 2016: http://www.abs.gov.au/ ausstats/abs@.nsf/mf/6291.0.55.003

2. Mission Australia Youth Survey 2016: https://www.missionaus-tralia.com.au/what-we-do/research-evaluation/youth-survey

Chapter 14

1. Saujani, R, 'Teach Girls Bravery Not Perfection', TED, Feburary 2016: http://www.ted.com/talks/ reshma_saujani_teach_girls_bravery_not_perfection

Bibliography

Abey, A and Ford, A, *How Much Is Enough?*, A&B Publishers, Sydney, 2007.

Anonymous, *Living with Teenagers*, Headline Review, London, 2008.

Apter, T, *You Don't Really Know Me: Why Mothers and Daughters Fight and How Both Can Win*, W.W. Norton, New York, 2004.

Benn, M, *What Should We Tell Our Daughters?*, John Murray, London, 2013.

Biddulph, S, *Raising Girls*, Finch Publishing, Sydney, 2013.

Carr-Gregg, M, *The Princess Bitchface Syndrome*, Penguin, Melbourne, 2006.

Carr-Gregg, M, *When to Really Worry*, Penguin, Melbourne, 2010.

Clark, L, *Beautiful Failures*, Penguin Random House, Sydney, 2016.

Cooke, K, *Girl Stuff: Your Full-on Guide to the Teen Years*, Penguin, Melbourne, 2016.

Darvill, W and Powell, K, *The Puberty Book*, Hachette Australia, Sydney, 2016.

Dent, M, *Saving Our Adolescents*, Pennington Publications, Murwillumbah, 2010.

Friedland, L, *Raising Competent Teenagers*, Rockpool Publishing, Sydney, 2014.

Fuller, A, *Tricky Teens,* Finch Publishing, Sydney, 2014.

Grant, I and Grant, M, *Growing Great Girls,* Random House, Sydney, 2008.

Haber, J and Glatzer, J, *Bullyproof Your Child for Life,* TarcherPerigee, New York, 2007.

Halphen, G [Ed], *Letter to My Teenage Self,* Affirm Press, South Melbourne, 2016.

Hawkes, T, *Ten Leadership Lessons You Must Teach Your Teenager,* Hachette Australia, Sydney, 2016.

Hinshaw, S, *The Triple Bind,* Ballantine Books, New York, 2009.

Huffington, A, *Thrive,* Harmony, New York, 2015.

Levin, DE and Kilbourne, J, *So Sexy, So Soon: The New Sexualized Childhood,* Ballantine Books, New York, 2009.

Locke, J, *The Bonsai Child: Why Modern Parenting Limits Children's Potential and Practical Strategies to Turn It Around,* 2015.

Mackenzie, RJ, *Setting Limits with Your Strong-Willed Teen,* Harmony, New York, 2011

Mann, S, Seager, P and Wineberg, J, *Surviving the Terrible Teens,* White Ladder, Devon, 2008.

McLean, S, *Sexts, Texts & Selfies,* Viking, Melbourne, 2014.

Miller, D, *Gratitude: A Positive New Approach to Raising Thankful Kids,* Inlumino Enterprises, Sydney, 2014.

Miller, D and Funnell, N, *Loveability: An Empowered Girl's Guide to Dating and Relationships,* HarperCollins, Sydney, 2014.

Mitchell, M, *What Teenage Girls Don't Tell Their Parents,* Australian Academic Press, Brisbane, 2011.

Orenstein, P, *Girls & Sex, Navigating the Complicated New Landscape,* HarperCollins, New York, 2016.

Osit, M, *Generation Text,* American Management Association, New York, 2008.

Palmer, S, *21st Century Girls,* Orion, London, 2013.

Paul, C, *The Gutsy Girl: Escapades for Your Life of Epic Adventure,* Bloomsbury USA, New York, 2016.

Preuschoff, G, *Raising Girls,* Finch Publishing, Sydney, 2004.

Reischer, E, *What Great Parents Do: 70 Simple Strategies,* TarcherPerigee, New York, 2016.

Rapee, M, et al, *Helping Your Anxious Child: A Step-by-Step Guide for Parents,* New Harbinger Publications, Oakland, 2008.

Sandberg, S, *Lean In,* Knopf, New York, 2014.

Senior, J, *All Joy and No Fun,* HarperCollins, New York, 2014.

Siegel, DJ, and Payne, T, *The Whole-Brain Child,* Scribe, Melbourne, 2012.

Sparrow, R, *Ask Me Anything,* UQP, Brisbane, 2015.

Witt, S, *Teen Talk Parent Talk,* Collective Wisdom Publications, Melbourne, 2011.

Acknowledgements

Almost two hundred 14-year-old girls made this book possible. They are anonymous in print, but that shouldn't diminish the remarkable insights they provided along the way. Across the country, they bared their souls in the hope that we – their parents – will listen to them. They want us to understand their lives, and how they still need us even if they don't know how to articulate that. They trusted me to tell their stories, to shine a light on their challenges, and I hope I've done that justice. Thank you girls; you've taught me so much.

So have their school communities; their principals, teachers, school nurses and guidance officers. For hours and hours, over weeks and then months, I sought the expertise of this group in the hope of painting a full picture of our 14-year-olds, and the challenges they face.

They responded with a generosity of spirit and time. Marise McConaghy, Flo Kearney, Jody Forbes, Kim Kiepe, Fran Reddan, Karen Spiller, Julie Warwick, Maree Herrett, Amanda Bell, Judith Tudball and Tony Freeman were among the dozens of school principals, education experts and school psychologists who provided guidance. So did Helene Hardy and Alex Curtis. Kids Helpline's Tony Fitzgerald, the Triple P's Alan Ralph, James Scott, Maggie Dent, Andrew Fuller, Michelle Mitchell, Susan McLean, Chris Seton, Dannielle Miller and Paul Dillon saw the importance of this project and generously lent their expertise. So did many others: Nicky Kozlovskis and Pauline Love from Mothers of Only Girls, Loren Bridge and many others from the Alliance of Girls' Schools Australasia, Melissa Kang, Judith Locke, Mia Freedman, Tracy Trinita, Caroline Paul, Veronica Howarth, Mark McCrindle, Kyla Wahlstrom, Saul Eslake, Garry King, Arun Abey, Andrea Cincotta, Catherine O'Sullivan and Robyn Kronenberg. Many people – particularly principals and teachers – wanted to remain anonymous, but provided their advice freely in the hope we all understand our 14-year-old girls a touch more. A driving passion to see how girls grow into awesome women was the motivation behind everyone's contribution. I hope I have provided a view that taps into all your expertise.

Writing a book is a big commitment, and it's always a team effort. My publisher Vanessa Radnidge believed in this project from the moment I raised it, and her enthusiasm knows no bounds. My editor Susan Gray asked me the questions that led to better answers, and Tom Bailey-Smith ensured it read like it should. Thank you. To all the team at Hachette – Lydia Tasker, Louise McLean, Jacquie Brown, Christa Moffitt, Isabel Staas, Fiona Hazard, Louise Sherwin-Stark and Justin Ractliffe – this has been a thoroughly enjoyable journey.

Finally, to my team: girlfriends whose own parenting journeys provide an underground advice club, and to my husband David Fagan, who is my partner in love and parenting, thank you. I've left a copy of this on your side of the bed. You should read it before our first turns 14.

Index

Resources

If you or your daughter are in difficulty, or just need someone to talk to, there are people who can help.

UK Resources:

Childline
childline.org.uk or 0800 1111

Parenting and Family Support
familylives.org.uk or 0808 800 2222

Samaritans
samaritans.org or 116 123

Young Minds
youngminds.org.uk or 0808 802 5544

Australia and New Zealand Resources:

Kids Helpline Australia
kidshelpline.com.au or 1800 55 1800

Kidsline New Zealand
kidsline.org.nz or 0800 54 37 54

Lifeline Australia
lifeline.org.au or 13 11 14

Lifeline Aotearoa
lifeline.org.nz or 0800 543 354

beyondblue
beyondblue.org.au or 1300 22 4636

National Depression Initiative New Zealand
depression.org.nz or 0800 111 757